Magical Power
For Beginners

© Marshall P. Reyher

About the Author

Deborah Lipp was initiated into a traditional Gardnerian coven of Witches in 1981, became a High Priestess in 1986, and has been teaching Wicca and running Pagan circles ever since. She has appeared in various media discussing Wicca, including the A&E documentary *Ancient Mysteries: Witchcraft in America*, on MSNBC, in *The New York Times*, and in many smaller TV and print sources.

Deborah has been published in many Pagan publications, including *Llewellyn's Magical Almanac*, *Pangaia*, *Green Egg*, *The Druid's Progress*, *Converging Paths*, and *The Hidden Path*, as well as *Mothering Magazine*. She has lectured at numerous Pagan festivals on a variety of topics.

Deborah lives just outside New York City with her spouse, Melissa, and an assortment of cats. She is the proud mother of Arthur Lipp-Bonewits. Deborah is obsessed with logic puzzles, James Bond, and old musicals.

Magical
Power

For Beginners

How to Raise & Send Energy
for Spells That Work

Deborah Lipp

Llewellyn Publications
Woodbury, Minnesota

FIRST EDITION
First Printing, 2017

Cover design: Kevin R. Brown
Interior illustrations and photo: Llewellyn Art Department

Llewellyn Publications is a registered trademark of Llewellyn Worldwide Ltd.

Library of Congress Cataloging-in-Publication Data
Names: Lipp, Deborah, author.
Title: Magical power for beginners : how to raise & send energy for spells that work / Deborah Lipp.
Description: First Edition. | Woodbury : Llewellyn Worldwide, Ltd, 2017. | Includes bibliographical references and index.
Identifiers: LCCN 2016056367 (print) | LCCN 2017006558 (ebook) | ISBN 9780738751986 | ISBN 9780738752433 (ebook)
Subjects: LCSH: Magic.
Classification: LCC BF1611 .L48 2017 (print) | LCC BF1611 (ebook) | DDC 133.4/3—dc23
LC record available at https://lccn.loc.gov/2016056367

Llewellyn Worldwide Ltd. does not participate in, endorse, or have any authority or responsibility concerning private business transactions between our authors and the public.

All mail addressed to the author is forwarded, but the publisher cannot, unless specifically instructed by the author, give out an address or phone number.

Any Internet references contained in this work are current at publication time, but the publisher cannot guarantee that a specific location will continue to be maintained. Please refer to the publisher's website for links to authors' websites and other sources.

Llewellyn Publications
A Division of Llewellyn Worldwide Ltd.
2143 Wooddale Drive
Woodbury, MN 55125-2989
www.llewellyn.com

Printed in the United States of America

Other Books by Deborah Lipp

The Elements of Ritual:
Air, Fire, Water & Earth in the Wiccan Circle
(Llewellyn, 2003)

The Way of Four:
Create Elemental Balance in Your Life
(Llewellyn, 2004)

The Way of Four Spellbook:
Working Magic with the Elements
(Llewellyn, 2006)

The Study of Witchcraft: A Guidebook to Advanced Wicca
(Red Wheel/Weiser, 2007)

The Ultimate James Bond Fan Book
(Sterling and Ross, 2006)

Merry Meet Again:
Lessons, Life & Love on the Path of a Wiccan High Priestess
(Llewellyn, 2013)

Tarot Interactions:
Become More Intuitive, Psychic & Skilled at Reading Cards
(Llewellyn, 2015)

Dedication

Holy Goddess Brigid, Lady of Creativity,
I offer this creative work to you.

And in Memorium

To Carl Llewellyn Weschcke, 1930–2015

contents

exercises and figures

Exercises

Figures

acknowledgments

This book rests on the shoulders of my wonderful magical teachers, especially Susan Carberry and Isaac Bonewits. It is unlikely I'd know much without them. This book is also a gift to me from everyone I've ever worked magic with or worked magic for. Every spell has taught me something important. I cannot begin to enumerate every spell I've done or every magician I've worked with!

As a start, I owe thanks to every former and current member of Rowentrye Coven, Stormcircle Coven, and Coven of the Dark Waters. I owe thanks to innumerable women with fertility concerns, soldiers who needed protection when going off to war, job seekers, cancer patients, AIDS patients, and others who reached out to ask for help. Asking for help is brave, and I thank you.

I particularly acknowledge Joseph Hull and Orien Rose Laplante. These two wonderful people survived devastating, horrific accidents as children—survived in part due to the hard work of many dedicated magic workers—and have grown up strong. Seeing them now gives me faith in the work I do.

I also acknowledge my wonderful son, Arthur Lipp-Bonewits. He gets a checkbox for a bunch of these thanks—I worked fertility magic for myself in order to get him, he was the subject of a number of spells at various points in his life, and he was a participant in spells as well. As a teenager, he faced an illness so thorny and complex that it took six different doctors and three different spells before he could get diagnosed and treated. He's also an expert on angels, and I reached out to him when angels and archangels were mentioned in this text.

Naturally, I also need to acknowledge the writing part of this process. My editors Elysia Gallo and Andrea Neff are everything editors are supposed to be—people who make writing better, and sometimes make it possible.

I also thank the wonderful group of people who were present for a ritual dedicated to Brigid performed in February 2016. At that time, this book was about 80 percent done, but I was facing an uncharacteristic writer's block and was just stuck. I opened myself up to Brigid's creative energies and promised to dedicate the completed book to her (which I have done).

Finally, to my beloved spouse, Melissa. Not just because I love her, nor because she's perfectly fine with me spending long evenings ignoring her so I can write, but also because our relationship is the result of not one, not two, but three spells. First, we each performed a spell to find a partner. Then we met each other and became friends, not recognizing who we were to each other or that we were the answer to those spells. Then we met other people and decided, separately, that *they* were the partner asked for in the spells. Finally, I performed another spell, at the end of which my "friend" came for a visit, and the rest is history.

introduction

This is a book about magic. It's about how to plan, construct, and perform magic, which is to say, how to do spells.

Some people say that magick with a "k" distinguishes occult magic(k) from the kind of magic done on stage with rabbits and saws and scarves. Maybe I'm a writer first and an occultist second, because I don't like purposely misspelling words to make a point. If you're flipping through this book to learn card tricks, let the bookstore owner or librarian know it's misshelved, and move along.

This book emphasizes how to raise and send power. These ideas, raising power and sending power, make up the bulk of the pages that follow—they're two of the necessary features of a spell. They're the features often missing from fictionalized magic, such as you'll see in a thousand movies and television shows. In fiction, all you need is magic words (which we'll discuss) and/or a magical object (which we'll discuss) and/or steps performed in the proper order (which we'll discuss). But rarely does fiction address the idea that you can have all these ingredients and there's still something missing.

Honestly, I think that omission is not so much a mistake as a potent fantasy. Make-believe magic is practically effortless, unlike real magic. In fiction, either some people are born Witches and others aren't (that's right, Harry Potter, I'm talking to you), or the same spells work for everyone and the only trick is in finding the spell and its ingredients.

In real life, though, magic requires effort, energy, and skill. Magic without power is a fancy car with no gas—it's really cool but it gets you nowhere.

In the pages that follow, we're going to talk about all the components of a spell, and that will include things like rhyming spells and other magic words, natural ingredients such as crystals and herbs, as well as spookier objects like wands and swords. But we're going to spend quite a lot of time on the parts of magic that don't appear on TV, things like altering consciousness, using rhythm, and the importance of focus.

I hope I didn't scare you away. I don't happen to believe that magic is hard work; in fact, I think it's a lot of fun. Magic is a craft, and like any craft, you get better when you work at it, whether you're creating beaded jewelry or throwing pottery or casting spells. But if I didn't enjoy it, I wouldn't do it, and I hope to convey to you the pleasure as well as the skill of casting spells.

How This Book Came About

About ten years ago, I wrote a book called *The Way of Four Spellbook.* That book is about elemental magic and elemental spells. It focuses on fire, water, air, and earth, and how to use them in magic. The book is 267 pages long, of which about thirty pages are devoted to spellcraft fundamentals—what is magic, what is power, what is a spell.

Now, one of the things I do is teach at various venues—Pagan festivals, bookstores, Pagan Pride Day events, and so on. Naturally, I've developed classes based on each of the books I've written. As it turns out, almost all of the teaching I've done related to *The Way of Four Spellbook* comes from those thirty pages of fundamentals. In fact, I offer a full-day intensive on spellcasting that is derived from that material.

So when I finished my last book, *Tarot Interactions*, and asked myself, "What's next?" I started thinking about my spellcasting material. What if I took those thirty pages and expanded them? What if I took that all-day intensive and made it into a book? That book is *Magical Power For Beginners.*

In truth, I'm rather frustrated with the dearth of magical knowledge I see among Pagans and Witches. With so much interesting stuff available online and in print, you would think that practitioners would have an encyclopedic knowledge of any subject that interests them, but I haven't found this to be the case. Rather, I see a tremendous need for the kind of information that's in *Magical Power For Beginners.* Incorporated into these pages are many of the questions I've been asked over the years, and many of the struggles I've witnessed are addressed. I've worked with an awful lot of magical people, exploring, in the course of workshops together, the spells they've cast that have succeeded, those that have failed, and those they are trying to figure out how to perform. All of that has made its way into this volume.

Ritual and Magic

Throughout this book, I will refer to your "ritual space," "altar," and so on. I have practiced Wicca for over thirty years, and the language of Wicca is a comfortable way for me to describe magic. However, there's nothing particularly Wiccan about this book or the magic we're discussing.

"Ritual space" can be wherever you practice magic. It is not necessary to magically create your space, or to do so in any particular way or as a part of any particular tradition. You can certainly do magic without doing ritual preparation of your space—I do so often—but there are advantages to preparing space ritually.

I see ritual as an act of magic. In chapter 1, I'll talk about "theurgy" as a kind of magic—magical working for or with God or gods. Regardless of whether your magic circle, temple, triangle, orb, or what have you is sacred or secular, the act of creating such a space from nothing is inherently an act of magic.

When I use ritually created space, I use a circle and think of it as sacred space. I'll say I "consecrate" the space, but you may prefer a less theistic word, such as "charge," "energize," or "create."

When I talk about an "altar," similarly I just mean a space at which you do magic. Maybe it's a religious and magical space. Maybe it's a table. Maybe you're working outdoors and you've wrapped whatever tools you need in a small cloth, and when you get to the place where you're doing your magic, you lay out the cloth and voilà! Altar!

At home, I practice magic in several different ways. Often I do so with my Wiccan group—my coven. Often I do so alone, or with my spouse. My altar might be the ritual altar used in coven meetings, but for a solitary spell it might be a square mirror I have set aside on a dresser for just such purposes. Or I might create a special altar just for a single spell, particularly if the spell needs to be set up and left there for a while.

Whatever works for you, in other words, is almost certainly going to work within the context of this book.

What's in This Book?

Before we get into the how-to portion, we'll explore some of the basics. What is magic? What do we mean when we use that word? How does magic work?

One of the things that makes magic work is *power*, but what else is there? Once we've covered that, we'll circle back to power and talk about all the various ways of raising power and then of sending power.

From there we'll talk about spell construction. What is a spell? What are the necessary ingredients of a spell? How do you incorporate all of this power you've been reading about into a spell?

Finally, we'll explore putting it all together. We'll talk about fine-tuning a spell to make it work in real life, and we'll talk about brainstorming the particulars of doing a spell. There are several real spells given as examples, including two spells presented side by side with the principles of spell construction, so you can look at the abstract and the practical together and see how one is informed by the other.

All of this is meant to empower you as well as your spells. For *creating* magic, it's all about you and *your* creativity. It's my hope that you'll feel free to experiment and give yourself permission to make mistakes—I've made plenty.

My son, Arthur, is a tap dancer. Once a year, my son's dance studio used to invite parents to come in and observe a class. In one such class, the teacher was showing the students how to do a step called a "shiggy bop." My son kept landing on his butt, but no one else was falling. The teacher said that Arthur was the only one who was doing the step right. The shiggy bop is *that* close to falling, and the only way to learn it is to land on your ass. The reason the other students weren't falling is because they weren't pushing their feet back far enough, they weren't pushing their balance off enough. It was only by taking the risk, letting yourself feel unbalanced, and falling, that you could learn the step.

To me, it was a great life lesson. Magic, like so many, many things, is a shiggy bop. You learn to succeed only by being willing to fall on your ass. Then, like the song says, you pick yourself up and try again.

Happy falling, reader!

one

What Is Magic?

Very few people enjoy sitting around and reading the dictionary, but every now and then a definition is a really handy thing. Lots of people talk about magic without asking the basic question "What is it?" Is magic defined by what is done? By *how* it's done? By who (magicians?) does it? Is it natural? Supernatural? (And what is "supernatural" anyway?)

We can start with the dictionary, with the understanding that the people who wrote it probably don't have much experience with real magic. Merriam-Webster gives us this definition:

magic = *a power that allows people (such as witches and wizards) to do impossible things by saying special words or performing special actions.*

This is a fictional definition, or at least a definition of fictional magic. It says that people can do impossible things, but impossible things *can't be done*. It also emphasizes the "special" words or actions, which, we'll learn, are so much window dressing.

Let's try Webster's Dictionary:

magic = *the art of producing a desired effect or result through the use of incantation or various other techniques that presumably assure human control of supernatural agencies or the forces of nature.*

This definition is a little snooty, with its "presumably," but it actually is a step in the right direction. I like that it's open-ended on the techniques, and I like that it addresses both the supernatural and "forces of nature."

Let's see what a real magician or two have to say. In his *Magick in Theory and Practice*, Aleister Crowley, the famous English occultist, said that magick (he liked the "k") is "the Science and Art of causing Change to occur in conformity with Will."

"Science and Art" is a great phrase, and many subsequent magicians have retained it. Magic is a science, with a reliable and, often, repeatable structure. It has underlying principles to be studied and understood. Magic is also an art; it often works intuitively and creatively, and the best magic gives practitioners the same sort of visceral feedback as other forms of creative expression. Just as a musician feels it in her gut when creating and again when performing, a magician is often working from a feeling, nonlinear place both when designing a spell and again when doing the magic. The work is both precise (science) and touchy-feely (art).

"Change in conformity with Will" sounds, at first, just like Webster's "producing a desired effect or result." There are, however, a couple of crucial differences. First, what Crowley meant by "Will" was "True Will," an esoteric idea found in his *The Book of the Law*. The meaning of True Will is core to Thelema, Crowley's mystical system, and is far more than simply what one desires. The True Will is, perhaps, one's destiny, or perhaps one's highest self, or perhaps one's desires when lived fully in accordance with nature. Like they say on Facebook, it's complicated.

The second important difference is that Crowley says "Change" and stops there, whereas Webster's goes on to say "through the use of ..." and tries to get descriptive.

If I determine that my True Will is to be in California, and I buy a plane ticket, go to the airport, get on a plane, and fly west, I have effected a change in accordance with Will. Is that magic?

By Crowley's definition, the answer is yes, and that's not an oversight. The real work of the Thelemic magician is in uncovering the True Will, and in creating change, however that change occurs. It's a definition that is meant to draw attention to the impossibility of separating magic from real life.

I'm all in favor of understanding that magic isn't separate from real life, a topic I'll return to. However, for a working definition of magic, muddying the waters with philosophy, however profound, doesn't really help.

Dion Fortune, the wonderful occult author and a contemporary of Crowley's, offered a definition that's even worse. She said that magic is "the art of changing consciousness at will." Once again, this definition omits any mention of *how* such change occurs, and makes matters worse by confining the change to "consciousness." Again, this is offering a definition that works better as philosophy than as linguistics. Fortune wants us to understand that, ultimately, "change comes from within." All change is change in consciousness.

Both Crowley and Fortune were involved with the "Great Work," which Crowley also called "knowledge and conversation of the Holy Guardian Angel." This is the work of transforming the self into its highest, and most godlike, expression, communing with one's inner divinity. The purpose of magic, both would assure you, is to achieve this.

They would also be adamant that a spell to get a job, change the weather, or win in court has nothing to do with magic as they defined it.

They would be wrong.

We haven't yet defined magic, but we're pretty close. We know that change is involved, and we have dictionaries suggesting that there is some kind of goal ("desired result") based on techniques that may be "impossible" or "supernatural" or something else.

So let's assume that when we end up with a definition, it's going to be in the realm of "XYZ techniques used to produce ABC results." Does it matter, then, if sometimes the results are profoundly spiritual and sometimes they're quite ordinary?

I'd say no.

In his book *Real Magic*, author, Druid, and magician Isaac Bonewits talked about "thaumaturgy" and "theurgy." These are Greek words for two kinds of magic: "wonder working" and "god working," respectively. What's important here is that, yes, these are two different kinds of magic, but they're both magic. As we proceed with this book, we'll talk about a whole range of techniques and methods, and the truth is, the same sets of techniques and methods apply regardless of the ultimate goal.

In chapter 6, we'll talk about "flavors" of power. You will probably want to vary how you raise power depending on where you intend to send that power—job-flavored power for a job spell, love-flavored power for a love spell. But that's tweaking the magic, not doing a whole different thing.

Let's use a food analogy. There are lots of different kinds of food with lots of different flavors. The food you prepare is geared toward a specific goal. My relaxing midnight snack of nachos is not my carbo-load before a marathon, is not my body-building protein shake, is not my celebratory birthday cake. But all of these are *food*, they're all prepared in a kitchen, and they're all digested. At a base level, they have more in common than not. Yes, they seem very different, but if you played "one of these things is not like the other," like they do on *Sesame Street*, and your choices were (1) nachos, (2) a plate of pasta, (3) a protein shake, (4) birthday cake, or (5) a shoe, you would not struggle to figure out which one doesn't belong.

In other words, magic is magic. Theurgy and thaumaturgy have also been called "high magic" and "low magic," respectively, and there is a centuries-long tradition of practitioners of one sneering at those who use the other. But the truth is, they're both doing the same things, albeit in different ways and for different purposes.

You can divide magic into all sorts of categories, of course. It's the old "there are two kinds of people in the world" game. There are *zillions* of kinds of people, which can be divided in a wide variety of ways. Magic can be divided into thaumaturgy and theurgy, into elemental attributes (as I did in *The Way of Four Spellbook*), into colors (as Bonewits did in *Real Magic*), into passive and active, or into any number of other groupings; and while these groupings are interesting and useful, creating groups like this never means that one or some aren't actually magic.

Let's go back to *Real Magic*. I learned a lot about magic from Isaac Bonewits, and was married to him for ten years, so it isn't surprising that I really like his definition of magic:

> *… an art and a science for dealing with particular types of knowledge, the manipulation of which will produce results that will astound and amaze the uninformed.* [1]

Bonewits then asks how magic differs from science, and concludes:

> *The science and art of magic deals with a body of knowledge that … has not yet been fully investigated or confirmed by the other arts and sciences.* [2]

---

1. Isaac Bonewits, *Real Magic* (Berkeley, CA: Creative Arts Book Company, 1971), 33.
2. Ibid.

I like this definition a lot, because it is the first one that tries to define the occult or supernatural aspect without going completely off the rails. Something is "occult" when it is hidden (the origin of the word) or unknown, or not fully known. Something is supernatural when it is outside of our understanding of how nature works. That understanding can, of course, change.

What I don't like about this definition, though, is the roundabout way it addresses the actual *doing* part of magic. It "deals with" knowledge, "the manipulation of which . . . ." Why don't you just *use* the magic?

In *The Way of Four Spellbook*, I defined magic as "the science and art of using occult and/or mystical and/or spiritual forces to cause change in accordance with will."

We're sticking with that. It's an *active* definition, emphasizing the "using" part; it references the occult and mystical while still leaving the definition of those things open, which is needed; and it makes clear that the purpose of magic is to produce a result. ("High magic" produces spiritual or psychological results. "Low magic" produces real-world results. In either case, we have results.)

In the following pages, we'll talk about all of this: the science and the art, the occult, mystical, and spiritual forces, the use of will, and causing change.

What Does Magic Do?

One of the useful things about defining magic is it tells us both what magic can do and what it can't do. We've gotten to a definition that says that magic uses certain forces—spiritual, occult, and mystical. It doesn't just *happen*; it uses something real, yet currently ill-defined, to make things happen. Bonewits says the occult is not "fully investigated" but leaves the door open for deeper understanding in the future.

When I first started teaching about magic, I lived in New York City (Queens, to be precise). I had a little spell I liked to do while waiting for the subway late at night. In those days, the subway ran every twenty minutes on its after-hours schedule. During the three years I lived in the city, using my spell, I waited more than ten minutes only two or three times—a statistically impressive feat!

But, I'd tell my students, doing the very same spell in the middle of a Kansas cornfield was really not going to work. Here's the rule:

Magic doesn't turn the impossible into the possible. Magic turns the improbable into the probable.

Because we're dealing with a whole lot of areas that aren't fully known, because all the knowledge in the universe isn't always at our fingertips, because medical science, physics, neuroscience, and other disciplines are still fraught with mystery, we can't always tell the difference between the impossible and the possible. (If we're not sure, it does no harm to do a spell that *may* be impossible!) Despite that caveat, this rule gives us a good idea of what magic can and cannot do.

Magic Can't
- Physically raise the dead
- Make people fly
- Make subways appear in the middle of Kansas
- Turn lead into gold

- Turn water into wine
- Etc.

Magic Can

- Heal the very sick, including those for whom medical science gives little or no hope
- Protect (a person, a home) from harm
- Make subways appear on subway tracks where they would have appeared eventually anyway
- Bring fertility
- Find missing things/people
- Get a job for an unemployed person
- Attract a mate
- Sell a house
- Etc.

How Does Magic Work?

Our definition gives us this very loose amalgam of forces that empower magic: occult, mystical, and spiritual. Can we get more specific? What is it exactly that makes magic work?

There are, it turns out, four specific things. Magic works because of the following components:

1. Interconnection
2. Transcending space and time
3. Intention
4. Power

Here is a short explanation of how magic works. We'll spend the next several chapters expanding upon it.

Magic works by (a) focusing your intention, (b) creating a direct path to the target of your work by using interconnection and by transcending space and time, (c) raising power, and (d) sending power toward the target.

Power

Power is the easiest of the four components to discuss, because we all pretty much know what it is. It may be hard to define in words, but it's easy to recognize. Whether we call it oomph, energy, or pizzazz, power is that buzzing, thrilling force that animates the inert, enlivens the blah, and brings a kind of wakefulness. When you're there and you feel it, you know it. We've all had those moments in life—maybe at a great concert, or during sex, or even in a quiet moment out in nature—when we've thought, "If only I could bottle this!" You feel the power coursing through the moment, and you know that if you could plug into it, you could keep a city's lights on!

Raising power and sending power are all about plugging into the source of that power; "raising" is generating the power and "sending" is directing it in such a way as to make it useful. After all, a thunderstorm is full of power, but it doesn't keep the lights on, because it isn't plugged in—the "sending" is missing.

The next chapters will be about intention, interconnection, and time and space. Once we've thoroughly explored these other components that make magic work, we'll return to the subject of how to raise and send power.

What Is a Spell?

It may strike you as curious that we've discussed magic for several pages now without ever discussing spells. Perhaps this is why the *Real Magic* definition of magic was a little indirect. Magic is a force, a principle, an understanding, a philosophy: a science and an art, as several definitions we looked at agree. But spells are the things that use magic.

> *A spell is a series of steps taken to achieve a magical goal.*

Chapters 8 and 9 are where we are going to define those steps in detail and dig into how to construct and perform a spell, how to fine-tune your magical work, what the specific components of a spell are, and more. But it would be odd to enter into chapter after chapter of how magic works without at least *mentioning* spells.

Earlier we used a food analogy, comparing magic to food. I prefer a slightly different analogy, still food-related: if magic is cooking, a spell is a recipe. I love this comparison because cooking, too, is both a science and an art. As a science, cooking uses chemical changes triggered by variations in temperature, by combining ingredients, by friction, and so on. The science part requires precise timing, exact temperatures, and controlled conditions in the kitchen. The art, though, requires creativity above all, a feel for what might work, an openness to experimentation, and a certain joie de vivre.

In cooking, we sometimes use recipes from books, or the Internet, or memory, and we sometimes make it up as we go along. In truth, making it up is also a recipe—one that's being written on the fly. In theory, you could certainly write down your spontaneous steps as you invent them, and then you'd have a recorded recipe for future use. Of course, you could also use a written recipe and change it—with substitutions, with different proportions, and so on.

Let's go back to the science and art of magic. In the analogy, spells are recipes. Indeed, there are many spellbooks on the market, just as there are many cookbooks. There are also "cookbooks" that are really in the business of teaching you how to cook and use specific recipes as lessons or examples, and there are spellbooks like that as well (*The Way of Four Spellbook* is one).

Fictional magic places a great deal of emphasis on spellbooks; we often "learn" in fiction that all you need to perform magic is the right spell from the right book, or that you need some additional gift or skill, but the spell is a necessary precursor. In reality, just as some people do fine in the kitchen without a cookbook, a magician can work without a spellbook. Raising and sending power, focusing intention, and establishing connection are absolutely necessary; opening the magic scroll and reciting the words will never be enough, and will never be strictly necessary either.

Why, then, use a spell? Well, as I've said, when you organize your magic into a series of steps, that *is* a spell, whether you used one from a book or made it up on the spot. Using a pre-written spell from an outside source can be inspiring and helpful, but anytime you put your steps together, anytime you figure out *how* you're going to do magic in any kind of linear way, you're creating a spell.

A spell is a series of steps taken to achieve a magical goal. Those steps, in their most basic form, are *(1) focus your in-*

tention, (2) create your connection, (3) raise power, (4) send power, and *(5) finish the spell.*

Why are spell "recipes" so much more intricate than this? First of all, they aren't, or they don't have to be. Creating the connection can be complex, and generally, most of the steps of a spell are working toward that goal. The connection, though, really helps with the focus quite a lot, so it serves multiple purposes. Additionally, multiple steps add different sources of power to a spell, as we'll learn.

When you've finished reading this book, pull a spellbook off your shelf (or off a bookstore shelf, if you don't have one) and see if you can determine, for any spell, which of these five steps correspond to the steps of that spell. Sometimes a spell may assume a step—the text may never tell you to focus, or when to send power. But having read *Magical Power For Beginners*, you should be able to fill in the blanks.

two

Everything Is Connected
to Everything Else

In the previous chapter, I told you that one of the ways that magic works is through *interconnection*. Fortunately, everything is connected to everything else. (I say "fortunately" because it makes magical interconnection so much easier to find!)

This is a spiritual truth that we all know deep down. As much as we may feel isolated and alone at times, we also sense somehow that we are connected. From the Zen master talking about being "one with everything" to philosopher Martin Buber talking about "I and thou," religion and philosophy, in the East and West, are replete with this paradox that we are isolated, yet we are all a part of one another.

Western monotheistic religions might argue that God is the connector, that we are apart from one another except through God. Pagan religions tend more toward *pantheism*, the belief that everything is God and there is no difference between God and the universe, or *panentheism*, the belief that God, or the gods, or some divine force, interpenetrates everything in the universe (but is not identical to it). Any of these could be termed a form of *monism*, the belief in the essential unity of all things.

Experiencing Connection

As a general rule, most of us don't experience our connection to the universe, to God or the gods, or to one another as a day-to-day thing. We feel like singular individuals, and sometimes painfully so. Often, our primary partnership (if we have one) is our one place of deep connection, and even there, we can feel the vast distance that separates us from another human being. If we are single, then we may attach fantasies of connection to the hope for love—blending the romantic and the spiritual.

Some of us deepen our feelings of connection through prayer, or ritual, or through time spent in nature. Some of us meditate. Feeling our connection to other human beings, to other living animals, to plants and nature in general, to the universe, to the mysterious, can make us happier, more content, and more at peace.

The philosophically oriented might say this *is* magic. In a way, they'd be right. It's certainly a form of "knowledge and conversation of the Holy Guardian Angel."

If we are seeking to understand and experience interconnection, we can't expect to just turn that experience on like a switch. We can meditate on it, and meditation is a helpful magical tool—one that will be discussed in chapter 4. We can also explore specific ways in which we can find connection.

Why *are* romance and spirituality intertwined? Simply put, it's because when we experience oneness with one other human being, we experience the potential for a vaster oneness. Either oneness is impossible or it's possible, and the moment we experience that extraordinary "click" with a partner, we know that it's possible. It becomes possible, then, with everyone. Most of us have felt that—falling in love and then suddenly loving the neighbor, the bus driver, the sky … everything. Because suddenly we're connected.

Love, in other words, is a way of experiencing connection. The Hindus would call this *bhakti yoga*—the yoga of love. Bhakti yoga teaches that a single love (for a spouse, for a child, for a parent or friend) can be used to lead us to the love of God and therefore to higher consciousness—in other words, to oneness.

The Road Map of Interconnection

This is a practical, how-to sort of book, but our brief foray into the spiritual and philosophical has yielded a powerful lesson. A single connection can lead us to more and more connection. Feeling a part of one human being can make us feel a part of all humankind.

Although we can see that the universe is all one, it's not an undifferentiated glop. At some deep level, everything connects, but in our day-to-day lives, we exist in a world in which things are different from other things, in which cars are not bunnies and toasters are not fireflies. How, then, can connection be perceived?

Interconnections can be seen between all manner of disparate things, like a road map—tangled routes and byways, odd little paths and massive superhighways. Eventually we can find the route between any two things. Like the game of "six degrees of separation" (or "six degrees of Kevin Bacon"), we can find a path through which any two (or more) things, beings, people, states of mind, goals, events, and natural forces connect.

In magic, we will then travel those paths.

The reason that any of this matters, for the purposes of this book, is because magic leverages interconnection to bring you and your target together. Interconnection is one piece of magic—if you recall from the previous chapter, I identified four components: (1) interconnection, (2) transcending space and time, (3) intention, and (4) power.

Let's assume that you want to do magic to make me rich. I'd love that! But you can't just decide to make me rich. You have to find a way to connect to me. You have to figure out the path from you to me.

On a road map as entangled as The Whole Universe, there are many routes between any two points. Your task is to figure out one or more routes, to connect us as deeply as possible.

I said one or more. That's where our road-map analogy breaks down, because we don't want just the one fastest route from you to me. It's *not* a road. When we connect to the subject of our magic, it's more like sewing—more threads make for stronger fabric, and each connection is a thread.

Physical Connection

The simplest way to form a connection is physically. I am connected to that which I touch.

In a traditional Wiccan consecration, part of consecrating something is to touch it to an already consecrated thing of the same type. Use a consecrated athame (a Witch's blade) to consecrate a new blade. Use a consecrated wand to consecrate a new wand—and make sure they touch. In general, there's much more to a consecration than just the touch, but the touch is an important part. Touching the new wand to the old wand *connects* it to consecrated "wandness."

The laying on of hands is a form of magic that utilizes touch. You magically heal a person by physically touching that person. With some forms of magical in-person healing, the practitioner does not touch the patient's body—the hands may rest a few inches from the patient's skin. However, the practitioner is "touching" the patient's aura—the invisible field that is an extension of the physical body. You could almost say this is trans-physical touch and is a form of physical connection.

Touching is one kind of physical connection. Presence is another—if we're in the same house, we're connected. In the next chapter, we'll explore the subject of transcending time. For now, though, let's assume that we can sometimes set aside time when we talk about physical presence. If you and I have been in the same house at different times, that's a connection. Connecting through presence and outside of time is one way that people sense ghosts or presences—people who were in the same place in the past may leave a resonance of themselves behind, even if they're not actually haunting the place. More mundanely, if you come to my apartment and sit in my favorite chair, you may get a feeling of "me-ness" even if I'm not home.

Concrete remnants, mementos, and components are a form of physical connection. In *The Way of Four Spellbook*, I describe a spell I did to get a home. I picked up a stone from the place where I wanted to live, and worked my spell using that stone. The stone was a physical part of the property I was targeting and therefore was connected to the whole. A lock of hair, given as a romantic gift, is a way of saying, "Here is a physical connection to me. I am present with you through it." Hair, nail clippings, pieces of jewelry, or articles of clothing worn by the target are often used in magic directed at a person.

As we delineate things that form connections, you can start to see that connections can be direct or indirect. You can touch me (directly) or you can touch something I touched (an indirect connection). Once you see that indirect connections are effective, you can understand those old spellbooks that call for the dust of someone's footprint and the like. The dust of my footprint is only one degree of separation from me, so it's way ahead of Kevin Bacon!

Magical Contagion

One of the basic principles of magic is that connection is *contagious*. Put a child with chickenpox in a classroom and you'll end up with twenty cases of chickenpox. Diseases are contagious through the air, through touch, or through fluid exchange, depending upon the disease.

Magic is considered to be contagious by touch, so magical contagion is a subset of physical connection.

"Magical contagion" means that *anything that was once in contact with someone or something is still connected to that person or thing.* This is what we've been talking about with physical connection—my footprint was once in contact with me and thus, through contagion, is still connected to me.

Magical Transmission

Another important idea is that *energetic charge spreads from the magical to the adjacent and similar non-magical.* This could also be called "contagion," but the word is already in use.

Suppose you charge up a batch of tea so that when you drink it you are better able to study. That's a neat spell for a student. You can mix in a small amount of your magical tea with a large batch of regular tea and now you have a large batch of magical tea! The regular tea was adjacent (touching, mixed in with) and similar (they're both tea).

The concept of magical transmission allows you to do magic that would otherwise be impractical. You could, for example, magically empower the fertilizer you're using in your garden, but a large quantity of manure might not be something you would want to bring to an indoor altar. A pinch, though, could be charged up and brought out to the garden, then mixed in with the rest of the stinky but potent blend.

Human Connections

Human beings have a unique set of interconnections that come from the "stuff" of being human, the community, family, and culture of humanity.

We are connected to our families, first of all. Since this is a "blood" connection, or, more accurately, a DNA connection, we could group it with the physical, but family has a human and cultural meaning as well.

In general, humans are connected by affiliations, and family tends to be among the most meaningful. Members of a coven are connected through that membership and often can easily work magic for one another by accessing that tie. Affiliation can be through the company you work for, the type of work you do, the sports teams you root for, or the place you're from. Have you ever been far from home and met someone from your hometown? The sense of instant friendship may be fleeting, but it's real—you feel like you're *part* of something through that other person. At my day job, my home office is in Texas, and the only other person from the Northeast and I became buddies for no other reason than we related to each other as Easterners (and yet I married a Southerner!). I have a relative who has formed life-long friendships with a group of people who follow the same band, and it's certainly not unusual for fandom of some kind or another to be a tie.

People are connected through religion, ethnicity, age, orientation, and the school they went to. When you go on a date and you discover that you both love the same music, eat the same foods, and quote the same movies, your commonality isn't particularly meaningful, it's just a recognition that you are touching another soul. You're saying, *Look, here and here and here we are touching one another.*

In magic, it's not so much "let's touch each other" as it is "how can I touch you?" If you are making me rich, or healing me, or using magic to inspire me, then you have to find a way to make *me* present in your magic.

Many books of spells suggest forming a connection through the astrological element or sign of the subject. My sun sign is Taurus, which is an earth sign. Keeping in mind the concept that many threads create a stronger fabric, it's pretty clear that "earth sign" is a single thread, but "Taurus" adds another, stronger thread. And if I add my Moon and Ascendant to the Taurus Sun, the connection will be stronger still.

Synchronous Connections

A synchronous connection is one based on a space-time connection. If a group of people are in the same place together, they can form a "group mind" or a "mob mentality"—they can merge based on the synchronous connection, for good or ill. A concert audience is a positive example—people can feel like they're a single being when the music connects them.

In discussing physical connections, I touched on the idea that you might be in a physical space once shared by other beings. You may establish the connection through the object—the house you live in, the piece of jewelry you own— or you may establish the connection through the path you share—*intersecting* at that house, with that piece of jewelry.

People who were born at the same time or in the same place share such an intersection, as do people who happen to witness the same event. When you ask someone their memories of, for example, 9/11, they may have been a thousand miles away from where you were that day, but you both remember it (if you're old enough) and share the memory, the moment, and the emotion. You are *being there* together.

Symbolic Connection

Understanding that a connection can be symbolic is extremely useful for magic. If you can't connect directly to a person, you can connect to them symbolically.

For example, if you know that I am a Taurus, you can use an astrological glyph (♉) or a bull (a picture, a toy, or a figurine). These connect to me symbolically.

You know I'm a writer. Any book that I've written connects to me directly—it's mine, it has my name on it, and it's a part of me, just as a painting is a part of the painter or a wood carving is a part of the carver. But paper and pen connect to me *symbolically*—without being *my* writing, they are symbols of writing.

Sometimes we're not doing magic where the target is a person, or a known person. Suppose you're doing magic to get a job, for example. You're targeting the hiring manager of a particular company, but you don't know that person. Maybe you've managed to find out the person's name, or maybe not, but you can't get a picture, a footprint, or a location. You don't know the hiring manager's birthday. At this point, you can get creative in determining what *symbolizes* "hiring manager" as well as what might symbolize the company or your line of work.

When doing elemental magic, any symbol of an element connects to that element. So a candle connects to any magic that relates to fire and a seashell connects to any magic that relates to water, just as a feather symbolizes air and salt symbolizes earth. Of course, these are just four examples of a dozen or more potential such symbols.

Similarly, if you're doing planetary magic, then symbols, glyphs, and colors of the planet could be incorporated into your magic. For Mars magic, for example, the planetary symbol (♂), the color red, or a piece of iron could all be used.

Numbers can be worked into a spell in a variety of ways in order to access numerological sympathy: the number of ingredients in an incense or oil, the number of candles, the number of words in a chant or spoken charm, the number of repetitions of that spoken charm or of a behavior, etc. Because there is a variety here, you can make a spell resonate with two different numbers—perhaps four ingredients and four candles with five repetitions of five words.

In appendix A, I've provided several tables of correspondences useful in magic, including elements, planets, and numbers.

Sympathetic Magic

This is the right time to introduce a crucial principle for any magical working: *sympathetic magic*. The principle of sympathetic magic is this:

> *That which is like a thing* **is** *the thing.*

Here is the crux of all these different forms of interconnection. If you can bring to your spell something *similar to* or *connected to* the subject of your magic, then you *are* bringing the subject to the spell.

If that which is like a thing (or a person, or an idea) *is* the thing, then, for purposes of magic, a picture of me is me. A piece of me (a lock of hair, a drop of blood) is me. Something intimately connected with me (a book I've written, a check I've signed, an article of my clothing) is me.

So if you're doing a spell to make me rich, then having any of these things on your altar as you work will be like you're working on me *right there*.

Layering

Layering sympathetic objects and other connections is a way of increasing the power of sympathy—of making the fabric stronger with more threads.

In other words, once you've got a picture of me, there is no need to stop. The picture *plus* the book plus a candle in my astrological color would also work.

A magical object can be created with this layering effect. Having a pile of different things on the altar might confuse your focus, but bringing the sympathetic threads together in a single object can be powerful. For example, take the picture of me and paint the astrological symbols on the back. Then take a lock of my hair or a page from one of my books, and wrap the picture around it.

Finally, don't dismiss personal connection. If you're working in a group, then the person who knows me best is the one best able to connect to me. In this case, the powerful object you've created shouldn't be considered a substitute for that personal connection, nor should the personal connection preclude creating the object. Do both.

Imitative Magic

When I was first learning about magic, I was taught that the three most important concepts were *sympathetic magic, imi-*

tative magic, and *magical contagion.* Over the years, I've come to understand that imitative magic and magical contagion are subsets of sympathy.

You can look at imitative magic as *sympathy by doing.* Imitative magic is performing an action that imitates the desired result of the spell. The most frequently cited references in folk magic are fertility spells—in which, for example, you would have sex in a field at the beginning of spring in order to "teach" the field to be fertile—and jumping spells—also for springtime, in which you would ride a pole or hobby-horse and jump through the fields, thereby instructing the crops to "jump high" (grow tall).

Here is a fairly common spell that I've seen in two or three books (at least). The purpose of the spell is to reunite a couple who are experiencing a rift. Take two objects to represent the two people—such as candles, each in the color of the person's astrological sign (for sympathy). Perform the spell over a period of days, and each day move the two objects closer together until, on the final day, they are touching.

The imitative magic in this spell is obvious: the objects are imitating the behavior the lovers are meant to emulate. Just as the lovers are intended to come back together, the objects are coming closer and finally touching.

When my son was sixteen, he had a long illness that was difficult to diagnose. It was very scary, as over a period of weeks he saw six different doctors and went for at least that many tests at different locations. One of his primary symptoms was dizziness.

Early in the illness, before we knew how long-lasting or serious it was, we (our Pagan group, of which he was a member) did a spell to help control the dizziness. We focused on grounding and on feeling weighted down to the earth.

During power raising, with Arthur seated in the circle, as each of us was moved, we got up and put something on him: a drum, a statue from the main altar, a stone from the earth altar in the north, the offering bowl. By the time we finished, he was weighed down under a fairly large pile of stuff.

Again, it's not hard to discern the imitation here. By grounding him under objects, we were working to teach his body how to be grounded and solid on the earth. (The illness required two more spells, focused on different areas, before we were successful.)

On another occasion, my group did almost the exact opposite. During a spell to get someone a job, we started to perceive that our unemployed friend was depressed and finding it very hard to get moving. He felt really stuck. So we got up and started walking around, moving our own bodies to create imitative magic around the idea of moving and not being stuck.

As you can see, all of these imitative spells are active and physical. All of them imitate a desired behavior or quality. With imitative magic, you're not imitating the subject of the magic, you're imitating the goal.

For example, the subjects of these spells were newly planted fields (two spells), lovers, my dizzy son, and an unemployed person.

The fields were not imitated; the desired end result was. The lovers were imitated inasmuch as they started out separately, but soon the spell imitated the goal instead. Dizziness was never imitated, nor was stuckness.

Since imitation is usually active, it is often used as a part of power raising, and imitation can easily be combined with other types of sympathy. For example, in the "lovers reunite" spell, you can have the two objects have sympathetic ties to the lovers. I used astrological colors as an example, but they could be pictures or figurines, or you could carve names into the candles—any of these would be sympathetic connectors above and beyond the imitation.

The Purpose of Sympathy

Why are interconnection and sympathy so important to magic? In part, it is because of *intention*. We'll talk more about that later, but for now it's enough to know that it's hard to really intensely want something, and focus on it, if you aren't connected to it. This is why, for example, personal stories matter so much in politics. You can read all the statistics in the world, but when you hear a story about an individual affected by an issue, you *connect*, you care, and you pay attention. It is the same in magic: you have to care, so you have to connect.

On a much simpler level, your magic has to go somewhere. Many people "send energy" without any clarity about *where* they're sending that energy. This is like sending mail without an address. Maybe you'll get lucky and the letter will somehow get where it's going, but is that likely? When I was getting married, I had a bunch of invitations to mail. I had to track down a lot of snail-mail addresses to make sure each invitation arrived. The address was the means by which the "energy" (invitation) I sent arrived at its destination. It was the connection.

When creating magic, raising power is vitally important, but sending power is equally important. You cannot successfully do magic without both. And to send, you must first find some kind of "address."

Bringing someone or something forth so they are present in your magical work is one way of transcending space, and that leads us directly into the next chapter.

Most chapters have exercises to help you apply and build upon what you've learned. Don't skip the exercises, because they'll help make magic real for you, and give you some practical skills.

Exercise 1: Interconnection

Do you have a friend who lives far away? Someone you can't easily connect to by seeing them in the flesh? Map out all the ways you can connect to your friend using the information in this chapter about interconnection. Make a list, draw a chart, or create a diagram.

Exercise 2: A Sympathetic Object

Take some of the connections from exercise 1 and create a magical object representing your friend. The section "Layering" in this chapter should give you some ideas. You can keep the object on your altar to send warm feelings to your distant friend.

Exercise 3: Symbolism

Come up with a list of symbols that connect to the industry in which you work or would like to work. Could those symbols work to help you create a sympathetic object?

three

Time and Space

In chapter 1 we said that magic works, in part, by transcending space and time. Now we're going to delve into time, and then space, and figure out how we can achieve that transcendence.

Time

One of the things that empowers magical work is the ability to understand time as less fixed, and less linear, than it is normally perceived.

For people interested in the occult and in New Age thought, this isn't a new concept. Philosophers and thinkers reach into the laws of physics to explain that time isn't real, although physicists aren't always thrilled with how laypeople describe their science. My good friend who is both a physicist and an occultist tells me that magicians often mistake the philosophical or spiritual for the scientific if they don't have a strong understanding of the math behind relativity. And he's right—I don't.

In reading up on the subject, I find a variety of scientists disagreeing with one another: time is considered a controversial topic. Physicist Julian Barbour, author of *The End of Time*, says that time is ultimately an illusion, and reality is a series of "Nows" with no linear connection. Physicist Lee Smolin, in his book *Time Reborn*, argues that time is real, not an illusion, and is vitally important. Barbour says that it is *change* that creates the illusion of time, while another physicist, Max Tegmark, says that both time and change are illusions—nothing can change, because everything already *is*.

From the point of view of magical practice, it is very useful to work within the paradigm that time is indeed an illusion. Let's explore that concept.

In his book *An Anthropologist on Mars*, the late Oliver Sacks describes "Virgil," a blind man whose sight was surgically restored when he was about fifty years old. The chapter "To See and Not See" describes Virgil's tremendous difficulties adapting to sight:

> *"The real difficulty here is that simultaneous perception of objects is an unaccustomed way to those used to sequential perception through touch." We, with a full complement of senses, live in space and time; the blind live in a world of time alone. For the blind build their*

worlds from sequences of impressions … and are not ca-
pable … of simultaneous visual perception, the making
of an instantaneous visual scene. Indeed, if one can no
longer see in space, then the idea *of space becomes incom-*
prehensible.

A person who is blind approaches space in a linear way.
A room is *first* the door, *next* the chair, and *next* the coffee
table. People with sight perceive space all at once. The things
in a room have connections and relationships—"things to sit
on," for example, as a logical grouping—but they don't have
a necessary *order*. The attempt to switch from a linear perception to a simultaneous one was too hard for Virgil. It exhausted him, and he often resorted to touch so that he could
perceive as a blind man instead.

Trying to wrap your brain around simultaneous when all
you perceive is linear will *blow your mind*. It's just barely possible. Reading about Virgil, though, I had an inkling of how
time might not be linear either. We perceive linear time; the
order is past, present, then future. But I had a sudden insight
that maybe moments, "Nows," were chairs and couches and
shelf units that were all, somehow, *there*, and not linear at all.

You and I are time-blind and can only perceive the linear. But there's some instant, all-at-once view that we don't
see. Imagining being Virgil was a doorway for me, by which I
could understand the notion of time as illusory.

Scientists, philosophers, and occultists will all continue
to argue about time, because we're all blind. We're trying to
perceive past an inability to perceive.

How Does Transcending Time Affect Magic?

Why is it that transcending space and time makes magic work?

Let's assume that magical power is a form of energy, one currently unrecognized by science. If this is true, then the laws of thermodynamics apply to magic. The first law of thermodynamics tells us that energy is constant in nature. It doesn't go away; it is just converted from one form into another. This is known as conservation of energy. When we talk about raising power later on, we're going to talk about converting other forms of energy into magical energy (power), but for now, let's assume we have the power. Now what?

When we send the power somewhere, through space or time, the journey causes the energy to dissipate. Movement (through space or time) is kinetic energy, so *moving* our magical power converts some of it into kinetic energy—in other words, burns off some of the power. To me, the image is of a meteor burning up when entering the atmosphere—you can send a powerful, intense magical "meteor," but if it has too far to go, it's not going to be much of anything when it finally arrives.

So in order for all (or virtually all) of the magical power we raise to get where it's going, we have to be able to transcend space and time, obviating the need for all that movement.

One way we do that was discussed in chapter 2. Sympathetic magic tells us that *whatever is like a thing* is *the thing*. So when we have a sympathetic object in our ritual space, we have no need to send our energy over a distance—the subject of the magical work is present with us.

Transcending time means that the "future" is not distant; it's another "Now," and can be reached and affected from the present "Now" without having to travel in a linear fashion.

Let's go back to the living room furniture—I like that analogy, because I find it easier to visualize time as simultaneous when I compare it to simultaneous space, like my living room. In this analogy, "yesterday" and "next year" and so on are all components of a room: the couch, the floor lamp, the coffee table, the TV stand. They can be perceived in any order, so they can be reached in any order. It is as easy to touch today/the couch as it is to touch yesterday/the floor lamp or tomorrow/the coffee table.

If it's all simultaneous, then I can send my magic to the future without sending it along a linear path. It doesn't have to go *through* Monday, Tuesday, and Wednesday in order to affect an outcome on Thursday.

Here's an interesting thing: If we can use our understanding of time as simultaneous to affect the future, we can also use it to affect the past.

There are things about the past that seem quite fixed. Our memories are pretty solid. If your best friend died when you were ten and you were never the same after that, her death seems like something that can't be changed. And I'd tend to agree: it can't be changed—not because time is objectively real (the jury is still out) but because the memories and experiences of a whole lot of people reinforce the solidity of what happened in the past. Real life isn't a science fiction movie where you can go back in time and stop a car accident from happening and everyone's memories of the accident instantly disappear. Remember that magic can't do the impossible!

While the past can be touched, physical reality is a lot harder to change. Memories are physical—they are stored as groups of neurons—and many things that happened in the past have a physical reality that cannot be changed. The more solid and established something is, the harder it is to change magically (or non-magically, for that matter).

This means that most of what can be changed about the past is psychological in nature. We can heal the "inner child." We can bring present-day perceptions to the past, and allow that to heal us. You know that old saying "If only I could talk to myself twenty years ago, I'd tell myself ..."? Well, you can.

Here's another interesting thing about perceiving time as nonlinear: it completely alters how we can think about reincarnation. Instead of having "past" and "future" lives, we have many lives, many selves, living in different time periods, living *now*. Instead of thinking, "I once lived in the 1600s, and today I live in the twenty-first century, and someday I'll live in the thirtieth century," you can think, "I have multiple selves, including one in the twenty-first century, one in the 1600s, and one in the thirtieth century." While we normally think of the passage of time as insurmountable, simultaneous selves are no more (and no less) disconnected through time than they are through location (as if I had multiple "today" selves in Africa, the US, and Sweden).

The Final Frontier

The more we talk about transcending time in order to improve our magic, the more it seems we're describing space as genuinely insurmountable. The things that allow us to transcend time don't seem to apply to transcending space. With space, as opposed to time, we naturally understand that we can travel in any direction. It takes no special meditative or imaginative exercise to figure out that we can move our magic from one part of space—one place—to another. But that travel uses kinetic energy, burning off some of our magical power. How can we transcend this limitation, leaving our magic intact?

We can again look to physics, which postulates that space, although it seems to be invariable, actually has variation based on how it is observed. The problem is, not only is the math used to calculate this variation even more complex and hard to follow, but physicality affects perception. Without the scientific details, it's enough for now to know that those who measure space have recorded this variation—the world around us is not quite as solid as it seems.

As discussed when considering changing the past, a physical thing, which is agreed-upon to exist by many people, is hard to change magically. That pushes to the edge of impossible, and as defined in chapter 1, magic can't do the impossible.

How, then, can we do things like distant healing, which requires our energies to be sent a long distance? If my friend in California is sick, how can I do magic on her behalf from New Jersey, three thousand miles away? People do these sorts of spells all the time, but they rarely stop to consider how to transcend distance effectively. Often magicians just intuit the method without realizing it, and sometimes magicians figure out this is a problem, and analyze how best to solve it. But without *some* approach to this problem, your spells will dissipate without reaching their target, despite your best efforts.

One way to overcome space is, again, through sympathy. Julian Barbour talks about "Nows" being related in nonlinear ways. I mentioned this idea when I said that furnishings in a room could be related—"things to sit on" or "things that are blue" or "wood things," for example. Barbour, being a scientist, prefers mathematical examples. We can easily see, for instance, that prime numbers are a related mathematical group regardless of the order they're in. These nonlinear relations are a form of connection, as described in chapter 2, and sympathy helps to overcome space just as it helps to overcome time. If the target of your working is in your ritual space (because a sympathetic representation of your target is in your ritual space), then there is no distance.

So in order to do distance healing, I bring my friend in California to me—by making a poppet or having a photo of her, or what have you.

Ritual Transcendence

The space you are in can also, paradoxically, transcend space. When studying various forms of Witchcraft or magic, you'll find several explanations for why a ritual space is established prior to doing any magical work. Usually (but not always) the ritual space is a "magic circle." Author and poet Doreen Valiente, who is often called the "mother of modern Witchcraft," says:

> *The circle is drawn to protect the operator from potentially dangerous or hostile forces without, and to concentrate the power which is raised within. The latter, arising from the magic circle, is called the Cone of Power.*[3]

Gerald Gardner, truly the father of the modern Witchcraft movement, provides further insight:

> *[Witches] are taught that the circle is "between the worlds", that is, between this world and the next, the dominions of the gods....*

---

3. Doreen Valiente, *An ABC of Witchcraft Past & Present* (1973; reprint, Custer, WA: Phoenix Publishing, 1986), 64.

It is necessary to distinguish this clearly from the work of the magician or sorcerer, who draws a circle … and summons … spirits and demons to do his bidding, the circle being to prevent them from doing him harm …

The Witches' Circle, on the other hand, is to keep in *the power which they believe they can raise from their own bodies and to prevent it from being dissipated before they can mould it to their own will.*[4]

In these two quotes, a number of concepts are introduced, all of which are used by magical practitioners of a variety of traditions when creating ritual space.

First is the idea that the magic circle is protective. If the practitioner is in the business of raising demons (as Gardner asserts), then the circle keeps the demons on the outside of the circle and the magician safely on the inside. Valiente is less specific about what the dangers are.

Second is the idea that the circle functions as a magical container, concentrating the power until its eventual release. Both of these are very utilitarian concepts—keep the danger out, keep the power in—but there's a third concept: that the circle is "between the worlds." This has become a widespread idea. There are even a couple of Pagan conferences that use the phrase as a name.

What does "between the worlds" mean? Gardner suggests it is between the worlds of the living and the dead, between this life "and the next." If the circle is between the worlds, it's not in *this* world—which means it's not a part of normal space or time.

4. Gerald Gardner, *Witchcraft Today* (1954; reprint, New York: Magickal Childe Publishing, 1991), 26.

Well, that's neat, isn't it? If you can create a ritual circle that is not a part of space and time, then your ritual circle can be *anywhere* and *anywhen*. There is no space except the defined space (generally the four quarters, corresponding to the cardinal directions, plus the center), and there is no time. In my own circles, I ban the presence of any timepieces and even any discussion of time. Clocks are covered, wristwatches are removed, cellphones are turned off. By keeping time well away from the circle, we can leverage the place between the worlds to do powerful magic that transcends space and time.

We can look at the circle's relationship to space in two ways. First, we can perceive that there is no such thing as location in the circle, that the difference between California and New Jersey is meaningless because I am not in a *place*, I am in the circle. The other way to look at it is that the circle can be *anywhere*. In this sense, it's like astral travel: the circle moves through space while being outside it, without expending kinetic energy.

In either case, we can use sympathetic connections to connect to my friend in California. If we view the circle as "non-place," then the picture of her brings her to this non-place. If we view the circle as moving astrally, then the picture—the connection—brings us to her West Coast location.

Ritual creates its own sympathetic connection. All magic circles are like all other magic circles, so if rituals are being done in other places or have been done at other times, then your magic circle has a resonant sympathy with them. Coordinated magic, worked by many individuals in different locations, leverages this sympathy. My altar is like your altar, and we can connect through them.

Through the creation of ritual spaces such as the magic circle, we transcend space and time.

Magical Intention

In chapter 1, I outlined four things that make magic work, and now we've reached the third of these: intention.

To intend is not to want, to wish, or to hope. It is neither whimsical nor haphazard. One of the great powers of magic, and one of its great weaknesses as well, is that in order to succeed at magic, you have to know what you want.

In fact, most of us want something many times throughout the day, randomly, momentarily, or impulsively.

Sometimes our desires are conflicted. We want someone or something without intending to *act* on what we want. We want to have sex with a particularly desirable person, but we also want to preserve the integrity of the relationship, or avoid relationships in the workplace, or for some other reason avoid acting on that desire. We want to spend all our money on a fabulous vacation, and we also want to save up for a down payment on a home. We want to rest and put our feet up, but we also want to stick with our exercise program.

Other times, our desires are vague or confused. We want a better job, but as what? We want to write a book, or make a film, or paint a masterpiece, but we don't know where to begin or if we are really the writer/filmmaker/painter for the task. We want a relationship, but we know our past relationships have failed and we're not sure why. We have a sense that things could be better, but we're not sure how.

Later in the book, we'll talk in detail about the process of assembling a spell's ingredients. As this occurs, the magician is naturally examining what she will do, what energies will be raised, and what results the spell is intended to achieve. This is a great time to slow down and really examine the intention behind the spell. As we plan a spell, we can consider and reconsider exactly what we're doing, and why, and if it's really a great idea, so that by the time we enter into the actual magic, we are (ideally) quite sure of what we want, and that we want it.

Here is how I define magical intention:

> *To intend is to focus fixedly and consciously on a firm desire, with determination and with absolute confidence.*

Intention, then, is not just the determination to achieve a result that leads you to the decision to do magic. Rather, it is the act of mental concentration performed *during* magic. For example, if you do a spell to gain a lover, "intention" doesn't mean that your life must, day in and day out, during every waking hour, be focused on gaining a lover.

Obviously, the two must be aligned—you must have a firm intention regarding your result in order to be able to concentrate effectively during your working—but that doesn't mean that, outside the bounds of performing the spell, you have to maintain that concentration. This might actually be a relief to you if you've studied some New Age systems of creative visualization and manifesting desire that ask you to maintain the imagery 24/7. The advantage of doing a spell is that the concentration is *bounded*; it's needed within the boundaries of the spell's beginning and end.

Firm Desire

In order to apply your magical intention to a spell with the goal of, for example, gaining a lover—in order, in other words, to have "firm desire"—you must examine your life and understand whether or not you really, truly *want* a lover. Maybe you're just horny and lonely, but your life has no room for a lover right now. If this is the case, then a lover is not your firm desire—not your true intention. Your magic will thus inevitably screw up, either by failing to bring you a lover or by bringing you one when the time is wrong, causing the kind of havoc it's easy enough to imagine!

So, before the magic begins, self-examination is necessary to explore your firm desire. Suppose you're doing magic for a job. Is a job your firm desire? If your rent is due and your partner is annoyed with you, the obvious answer is yes! But many of us have complicated, mixed feelings about work. Maybe a part of you would prefer to stay home with the kids.

Maybe your inner teenager is rebelling against the need to work, even while your outer adult is actively job seeking.

Magician, know thyself.

"Inner work" is often considered to be entirely separate from magic. This is sometimes true—going to a self-help group, for example, is unlikely to be very magical. But here we see that in order to do magic, self-exploration has to reach past the surface desire, down into the subconscious.

Recall our earlier discussion in chapter 1 on thaumaturgy and theurgy. While the literal meaning of these words is "wonder working" and "god working," psychological work is generally grouped under theurgy, since exploring the inner psyche and attuning to the higher self are not so very far apart. Now, you're probably not going to do theurgic magic every time you think you want to do some thaumaturgy. My point is that exploring your inner self has a long magical history. And besides, it's necessary.

Knowing your *firm desire* is the part of that necessity under discussion at the moment, but inner work will impact other parts of magical intention as well, notably fixed focus and absolute confidence. Self-trust is something most of us achieve only after really digging deep and exorcising inner demons of doubt. Focus, too, requires an ability to plumb the depths of consciousness and unconsciousness, undistracted by unexplored territory.

In truth, there are a lot of magicians who think that the occult is a means of avoiding purely psychological explorations. I've met occultists who think of themselves as "above all that." But the most powerful magical people I know, people I'd trust to heal or help me, are people who've explored themselves through a variety of modalities. These are people who can comfortably discuss the current issues they're process-ing, who are unashamed to reveal their struggles and eager to share their discoveries. There is a great bravery there that serves them well in their magical lives.

Fixed and Conscious Focus

To "focus fixedly and consciously" is to maintain a clear im-age or idea in your head for a sufficient length of time. It re-quires a disciplined mind. Later, we'll learn spell techniques that make focus easier, but none of that will work without first developing proficiency in basic mind skills.

Fixed focus means that your subject matter doesn't wa-ver. If you're looking to make me rich (an excellent goal), then focusing a little on me and a little on someone else isn't ideal. If you think about making me rich and then allow your mind to wander, because chocolate is rich and there's that cute guy named Rich, and oh yeah, where was I?—then your lack of focus will undermine your ability to accomplish any-thing magically.

There is such a thing as accidental magic. Some people can have a fleeting thought of such ferocity that it makes its way to the target. Some people have natural power fields around them. For example, I have a friend who was known for break-ing things by walking near them. This sort of thing is kind of cool, and kind of spooky, and basically useless. It has no prac-tical application! Without *consciously* choosing to do magic, you're just throwing energies around—maybe they do what you desire and maybe they don't. Maybe they cause harm. Learning to focus your magic consciously will, as a happy side effect, help you to avoid sending power *un*consciously.

Determination and Confidence

When you focus "with determination and with absolute confidence," you know that you *can* achieve your goal, that you *will* achieve your goal, that you *already have* achieved your goal. That "already have" bit is really helped along by transcending time, as we learned in the previous chapter.

Doubt has no place in a magical working. Doubt pulls your focus away from the goal and places it in the "what ifs." When you focus with confidence, you leave no room for doubt.

Self-doubt is pernicious. You may have been reading this chapter and thinking, "I'll never do that" or "I can't succeed at that" or "I'm so easily distracted." Set "never" aside. Of course you can do it! Mind skills are developed through study and practice and through recognizing that you are not an automaton.

I have to say, I often *feel* very distracted and distractible. My mind wanders in conversation, and sometimes I get incredibly restless when I'm working. Even while writing this, I have a game of solitaire open, and I keep flipping back and forth. How, then, can I talk about fixed focus?

The answer is simple. I get the job done, and my internal experience is not the best gauge of how well I'm doing. By this I mean the game of solitaire gets played, yes, but the book also gets written, and the proof is before you. My self-critical thoughts are a poor measure of how hard I'm actually concentrating, of how much attention my writing actual receives.

Is there imperfection? Sure. "Fixed" focus doesn't mean "perfect, unwavering, never ever EVER distracted" focus. It means you maintain the fixed image and any distractions are dealt with quickly. Understanding that will build your confidence. Indeed, disciplining your mind has two purposes: the first, to learn how to focus, and the second, to give yourself confidence that you *can* focus. Both are part of magical intention.

Self-confidence comes from trusting yourself, and this calls back to our earlier discussion of inner work. If you do not trust yourself, then engaging in therapy or counseling or other work that creates self-trust will take your magic a long way.

Confidence, though, is also confidence in the magic itself.

The first part of magical confidence is overcoming the creeping inner suspicion that it's all bullshit. Let's face it, we're all a product of our culture, and our culture thinks the occult is a load of crap. Even if we were raised in a home that was more open-minded, we've been exposed from infancy to TV, school, friends, and so on, all of which may have been absolutely wonderful but still managed to instill in us a feeling of doubt that magic can be real. When we do magic, we must overcome that doubt, or at least set it aside. (By the way, upbringing definitely matters. Second-generation magicians, including my own son, approach the art with a great deal more natural confidence than those of us who were raised to be more skeptical.)

There is nothing wrong with skepticism—it's good not to be credulous! Investigate, examine, consider, and experiment. Don't take things—including the things you read here—at face value. Just because I say something, that doesn't constitute proof. But skepticism should be tempered by the possibility that the unexpected can be true.

If you doubt magic, doubt before or doubt after but do not doubt *during* the work. Doubt disrupts your confidence.

There are lots of techniques for setting aside doubt and distraction. Here are some ideas:

- Imagine the unwanted thoughts as pets that are bothering you when you're working, then just shoo them out. "Go away, Fluffy!"

- Imagine a room where unwanted thoughts live. Lock them in for the duration of the magic. You may put a twenty-four-hour timer on the lock, if you like.

- Wrap unwanted thoughts in a package and seal it up, giving yourself permission to open the package later.

- Slip unwanted thoughts into a pocket. This can be doubly effective if you wear special magical garb (robes, etc.) when you do your work, because the thoughts can be in the pockets of your day-to-day clothing.

Experience is the best way to conquer the doubt born of cultural bias against magic. As you see spells work, as you feel energy and its results, your confidence in the possibilities of magic will naturally increase.

I have found that performing just one spell that doesn't work can undermine my confidence greatly. Again, this is cultural. Because I was raised in a skeptical culture, with a predisposed inclination to believe magic doesn't work, I can have ten successes followed by one failure (or apparent failure) and spiral into the darkest of self-doubting funks. Here I must remind myself that even the greatest doctors sometimes lose patients, even the greatest of songwriters turn out songs that don't become hits, and even the most brilliant of scientists follow research down a dead-end path. Work can be valid at a success rate of less than 100 percent.

There have been times when I've found that apparent failures weren't failures after all. One time I participated in magic to cure a disease, which then lingered for six months. I doubted myself a lot until I discovered the normal course of that illness is two years or more. Positive experience, as I said, bolsters confidence, while negative experience can undermine it. I handle failed spells by giving myself permission to fail as much as a doctor or a songwriter does, and by noting the cumulative successes I have experienced over time, which greatly outweigh the failures.

Confidence and determination also apply to the specific work you're doing, not just to magic in general. You may have great faith in the power of magic to heal, but when presented with a request to knit a broken bone, your confidence may disappear. There is a fine line between the unlikely and the impossible, and often only you can decide which side of it a particular working lies on. If you feel you are attempting the impossible, if you look at the task ahead believing it cannot be done, then you cannot have true magical intention, because your confidence is absent.

One place where I often draw the line is distant healing for people I have not met and do not know. You see this sort of request all the time on occult- or Pagan-oriented e-lists and Facebook groups. "My Aunt Tilda is in the hospital. Please send energy." I don't know Aunt Tilda, I don't know anybody who knows Aunt Tilda, and I don't know what she looks like or exactly where she is. I have no confidence in my connection to her, so I don't do the work.

Because you are confident in your magic, it's important not to do anything to plant even a small seed of doubt. It is from here that the tradition arises that you must not talk about magic you have done. The "rule of silence" has various permutations. Some people say you must *never* talk about magical work you have done. Other variations of this rule are not to discuss it for twenty-four hours, or one moon cycle, or until you know for sure whether the magic did or did not have the desired result.

Remember that you are disciplining your thoughts to *set aside* doubt. As a product of your culture, as a thinking, rational being, it is natural that you will sometimes have questions, or feel weird, or wonder if the whole occult thing is some kind of delusion. Eventually you're going to let doubt out of its locked room, or pocket, or whatever. It's important to avoid putting energy into your magical work while that doubt is out and about.

Use your rational, analytical, doubting mind to study magic and to improve your skills. That includes reading books like this one and analyzing the work you've done once the rule of silence has been lifted. (I don't hold to the "never" version of the rule for this reason.)

Emotion

Many books on magic talk about the necessity of having strong emotion. Indeed, in talking about intention, both "determination" and "firm desire" suggest a certain level of passion is needed.

Strong feeling, though, has both pluses and minuses in magic. While it certainly helps you to want something badly, it can also make you irrational. The crazy feelings that can lead a person into a bad relationship, an impulsive move, or a stupid risk can lead them into ill-advised magic as well.

With firm desire in place, it is helpful to *work yourself up* into a passionate emotional state while doing magic. What's *not* helpful is to be so emotional that you are unable to determine whether or not magic is a good idea. Just because you still love your ex and want him back doesn't mean it's ethically right or magically sound to send energy toward that end. Magic done in the heat of anger can be powerful. The question is, do you want to live with the results? Anger also tends to splatter magic, and the chaos of its emotional intensity can send your energy in all directions instead of targeting it.

On the other hand, nothing is more powerfully connecting than love. When you deeply love someone, you can form a sympathetic connection easily and focus naturally. Love transcends time and space. A sympathetic object becomes secondary when someone is present with you because of the depth of your love (although it's still good to use one). I don't need a sympathetic object to connect to my son, my spouse, or my cat—they are with me always.

Developing Mind Skills

So, I've spent quite a few paragraphs telling you that you need mind skills in order to do magic effectively. How do you develop these skills? Let's talk about three things:

- Meditation
- Grounding and centering
- Visualization and sensory exercises

Although there are certainly more mind skills to explore, these three will give you a strong basis to proceed into more advanced exercises. Then we'll get into how to *practice* your mind skills.

More advanced skills, including trance, aspecting, creative visualization, and dreamwork, all depend on the skills described on the following pages.

Meditation

We have to talk about meditation first because without it, no other mind skill can be practiced effectively. Meditation is the training ground whereby you become able to do all these other, fancier things. Meditation is like a basic physical exercise program: it's good in and of itself, but it's also both a precursor for athletics and something every athlete continues even while performing more sophisticated physical feats.

Myths About Meditation

- It's hard.
- It's possible to "fail" at meditation.
- You're bad at it.
- It can only be done one particular way.

Let's start by exploding these myths!

All of these myths tend to come from the same place—an image you have of meditation that may not have come from a teacher at all. You may have heard about meditation, or seen it described, or picked up a cultural image somewhere or other—some TV show or comic book—and proceeded to try it yourself. You tried with the best of intentions, in order to improve yourself, to reduce stress or anxiety, to become wiser, or to deepen your occult practice. But eventually you ran into a problem: Your mind wandered incessantly, you fell asleep, you got itchy, you *completely forgot* you were meditating. You found lotus position impossible! You couldn't remember your mantra! *You didn't know what you were doing.*

Calm down, I'm here to help.

Why do I say that it's not possible to fail at meditation? If all these things happen—wandering mind, itchy body, snoring—isn't that failure?

In order to gauge the success or failure of anything, you have to understand what its purpose is. Generally, Western people are greatly misinformed about the purpose of meditation.

Things That Are Not the Purpose of Meditation

- To achieve nirvana
- To silence the chatter of the mind
- To become a meditation superhero

Here's the problem. The cultural image of meditation tends to come from one specific school of meditation (or one of several), with a very narrow purpose. It is true that a Zen Buddhist or a Hindu yogi might sit in meditation in order to achieve enlightenment. It's *also* true that such meditators practice daily, for decades, in the hope of finding moments where the mind is utterly silent. *Decades* of practice for *moments* of silence. Please keep that in mind when you feel that your efforts are going nowhere. Such meditators are the equivalent of world-class athletes, and their meditation has as little to do with yours as the exercise of Olympic medalists has to do with your get-in-shape Zumba class.

One of the purposes of meditation is to become acquainted with the way our own minds work. You may think you already know that about yourself, but in fact, we rarely have the opportunity to simply observe our own minds. Either we're busy doing something or we're actively engaging with our thoughts, feelings, and fantasies.

What does the voice of your inner thoughts actually sound like? Is it always the same? Is there more than one? Is it different when you're in different emotional states? Different psychic states? What are the tricks your mind likes to play on you? What are its distraction techniques? What works and doesn't work to overcome those distractions?

One of the things that meditation is, is an opportunity to uncover answers to these things. Your mind is your number-one magical tool, so learning how it works is pretty important. It's fairly obvious, then, that you are not failing, and not "bad at" meditation, if what happens is you notice your distractibility.

But that's not all there is to it. The process of meditation is the process of observing your mind doing its thing while you then continue to do what you intended to do.

The example I like to use is my own writing. As already mentioned, I'm easily distracted and I like to play computer games. When I sit at my computer to write, there's always a game of solitaire that I could easily open or already have opened. There's sometimes music on. There are noisy upstairs neighbors. There are, in other words, all the distractions that a restless mind could hope for.

If I judged the success or failure of any given writing session on whether or not I noticed any or all of those things, then every single session would have to be judged a failure. Instead, I judge based on something simpler and far more reasonable: whether or not I wrote.

As long as I am writing, I am successfully engaging with my own distractibility, I am being with the distractions, noticing them, and letting them go long enough to focus. In fact, I write with *intention*. I focus fixedly on my subject, I have a firm desire to write, I am determined, and I am confident. And the results are empowering: The book you hold in your hands is my eighth. With each book, I am more confident because I have experienced evidence of my own success. *Practice and experience improve intention.*

But what about the noisy neighbors? What about my itchy nose? Here's what I do: I notice them. Perhaps I pay attention for a moment or two. Then I go back to writing. Here's what I don't do: sit and listen to the neighbors and think, "Damn, I really should get back to my writing," then scratch my nose and think, "Damn, I really should get back to my writing."

Meditation is similar. The neighbors, the nose, the cat who lands in my lap and purrs the minute I light my incense and begin … All of these get a moment of thought. All of these allow me to briefly forget that I'm meditating. Then I go back to what I was doing.

If instead I petted the cat while thinking, "See? I'm bad at meditation," I would be succumbing to the distraction. When we think we fail, it's often because we *notice* the distraction, not because we *succumb* to it. But the thing is, noticing and then feeling bad about our own abilities is *just more distraction,* and ironically it's more likely to make us utterly succumb, at least for a few minutes.

So here's how it works: Notice the distraction and then just set it aside. Get back to meditation. Notice and, if it so happens, succumb, and then, as soon as possible, get back to meditation. It may be that, at the end of a twenty-minute session, you had three cumulative minutes of undistracted meditation. *That's great.* It's great for a lot of reasons: One, because being fully undistracted is hard, and any achievement is worthwhile. Two, because every achievement builds on previous achievements, so next time you're likely to get four or five minutes. Three, because you spent seventeen minutes engaging with how your mind behaves, and what that's like, and you began the process of learning how to quiet it and move on with what you were doing.

We all lose and return to focus all the time. We do it when studying, and at work, and even when making love. What we don't tend to do is to *be with* our inner thoughts and discover what that mechanism is.

As you become more skilled at meditation, you will find out that no matter how good you become at setting aside inner chatter and getting back to the meditation, you will never, or almost never, utterly silence that chatter. That's not how the ego-mind works. To sit *zazen* and still the ego-mind can indeed lead to enlightenment, and the ego-mind experiences that as death—to transcend the ego is, in a way, to kill it. Thus, the ego will resist like crazy—it has a survival instinct.

Since your goal is not to transcend ego but simply to discipline yourself for the purpose of improving mind skills, a little chatter is fine. Don't worry about it. As you learn the technique of bringing your thoughts back to the task at hand, you are learning how to focus fixedly during magic.

Preparing to Meditate

Regardless of the meditation technique you use—one of those described later in this chapter or an entirely different one—you'll do better if you take the time to prepare.

Have the Time and Space

Many of us lead busy lives, often hectic, often overscheduled. If you squeeze your meditation in between two highly scheduled blocks of time, the thought of your impending time limit is likely to be your biggest distraction. If one ear is open for the baby, you will not be able to dive deep into the experience. If you're a parent, get your partner's buy-in that these twenty minutes are entirely yours, and anything that arises is his or hers to deal with. And *stick to it*. If you hear something, assume your partner will handle it as promised.

One of the ways that people feel like failures at meditation is by falling asleep. Often this is because they're taking late night as their meditation time, and they're already exhausted. Meditation directly before bedtime isn't ideal.

The United States is a sleep-deprived culture. If you are tired all the time, then getting more rest is a more urgent need than learning how to meditate, and you should deal with that first. Meditate when you're sufficiently rested.

Have the Privacy

It's important, if you live with other people, to let them know you're meditating. If you're embarrassed by it, then you'll feel weird about getting "caught," and that's a distraction. Plus, letting others in the household know what you're doing prevents them from knocking on your door or yelling for you. Turn your phone off, lock your door, and figure out the best way to deal with your pets. (I don't lock mine out, because when I do, they scratch at the door.)

Have the Comfort

Constricting, binding clothing has no place in meditation. Again, you're reducing distractions—do you *really* want to be thinking about the belt buckle digging into your gut? For a seated or reclining meditation, figure out the position that works best for you. This may change over time as you try different techniques. If falling asleep is a problem, your position should help you avoid it. Don't meditate in bed if that's an issue.

And by the way, falling asleep, if you're not sleep-deprived and it's not bedtime, can be a way for your mind to do its work. If you fall asleep during meditation, maybe you're just tired, but maybe there was inner work to do that was best accomplished in a dream state. It happens.

I love to meditate in a hot bath. The privacy and pet-avoidance are built-in, I'm comfortable, I'm not going to fall asleep, and the hot water is physically relaxing. I can even add herbs, oils, or salts to my bath that promote the goal of my meditation (relaxation, awakening, opening the third eye, etc.).

Meditation Techniques

One misconception about meditation is that it's done one way and one way only: seated, preferably in lotus position, with eyes closed. A slightly more complex understanding of meditation includes that it might involve emptying the mind or it might include a mantra (a phrase to repeat). That's about the entirety of education on the subject you can get from pop culture.

In fact, there are many different ways of meditating, many different schools and traditions of meditation, and many different things that can be meditative.

Broadly, we can categorize meditation techniques as those that draw the mind inward, into an idea, into concentration, into listening or focusing, and those that push the mind outward, inducing a trancelike state.

Inward Meditation Techniques

Inward techniques require your thoughts or feelings to engage in a specific way.

Meditate on an Idea: A magical meditation—one that relates to this chapter—might be "What is my firm desire?" To meditate on an idea might seem the same as to think about it, but in a meditative state you have access to more of your mind, at a deeper level and with better focus. Meditating on an idea might be asking yourself a question, or reciting to yourself a favorite quote and exploring it deeply. Reciting a mantra can be the exploration of an idea, as can reciting a prayer.

Meditate on an Image: In Hinduism, both mantra and mandala meditation—focusing on a phrase or an image, respectively—can be either inward or outward techniques. When the mantra is an idea, it's inward. When the image is meant to be understood, it's inward. Icons of deities or other symbols are often the subject of meditation.

Meditate on a Feeling: While a prayer can be the contemplation of an idea (what does it mean when I say "the Lord is One" or "the earth is our Mother"?), it can also be focused on an emotional state: devotion, love, surrender, or feelings one may dive into during prayerful meditation. Buddhist "lovingkindness" meditation is a technique entirely dedicated to creating and deepening the feeling and experience of lovingkindness—toward yourself, your family, and the world.

Listening Meditation: In this sort of meditation, you focus on listening for inner wisdom. You allow your chattering mind to be sufficiently stilled to hear a deeper voice. You actively open yourself and listen—to deity, to your own higher self, to your ancestors, to nature, or to something else. For example, the following is a description of the meditation at a Quaker meeting: the community is silent, experiencing stillness and allowing each member to listen receptively:

> *The practice of sitting together in silence is often called "expectant waiting." It is a time when Friends become inwardly still and clear aside the activities of mind and body that usually fill our attention in order to create an opportunity to experience the presence of the Holy Spirit. It is not a time for "thinking," for deliberate, intellectual exercise. It is a time for spiritual receptivity, so it is important not to clog one's mind with its own busy activi-*

ties. Nonetheless, thoughts will occur in the silence. Some thoughts will be distractions and should be set aside. (Make that shopping list later.) But some thoughts or images or feelings may arise that seem to come from a deeper source and merit attention. If you are visited by a spiritual presence, if you seem to experience perceptions that are drawn from a deeper well or are illuminated with a brighter light, then let those impressions dwell in you and be receptive to the Inward Teacher. Each person finds his or her own ways of "centering down," or entering deep stillness during meeting.[5]

Outward Meditation Techniques

The majority of meditation styles by far are outward techniques. These are techniques that use repetition, rhythm, breath, sound, or movement in order to release the mind from normal thoughts and induce a deep, relaxed, and almost mindless state.

Breathing: Concentrating on your breathing is one of the most venerable meditation techniques. Common in yoga, it is often used in the West with no association to mysticism. My mother, a social worker, teaches "square breathing" to clients as a relaxation technique. (Square breathing is so-called because it is 4 x 4: inhale-two-three-four, hold-two-three-four, exhale-two-three-four, hold-two-three-four.)

There are a wide variety of breathing techniques. They concentrate your focus on the breath while moving energy

5. "Traditional Quaker Worship," Quaker Information Center, www.quakerinfo.org/quakerism/worship.

throughout the body. Breathing can be relaxing or enlivening, or both.

Repetition of a Prayer or Phrase: As mentioned previously, a mantra can be inward, focusing on the *content* of the phrase, or it can be outward, allowing the repetition to lull the mind. This technique works best with short or rhythmic sounds or phrases. "Om" can be used for both inward concentration—contemplating the meaning of a syllable that encompasses time, creation, and the universe—and, at the same time, outward release—allowing the resonance of the sound, the vibration, the deep breathing, and the simple repetition to alter consciousness. Vibration has measurable results on consciousness, and mystics believe that different sounds, each with its own vibrational frequency, have different effects.

Meditate on an Image: Again, this one is a repurposing of an inward technique. This time, the focus is on allowing the eye to journey through a geometric shape, away from thought or meaning. Meditation can be done by gazing at the image or by drawing or tracing it. Coloring mandalas is increasingly popular as a modern meditation technique.

Movement Meditation: An acquaintance with restless legs syndrome tells me she is able to meditate only when she walks. Walking can be simple and rhythmic, allowing your thoughts to center themselves in your body, in the physical sensation of movement, in the tempo of your steps, and in the nature of your surroundings. The walk itself can be meaningful, such as walking a labyrinth.

Mandalas and labyrinths can also be traced by hand (I've done this with a labyrinth about two-feet square), which makes this technique accessible to people with mobility issues. Movement doesn't have to involve the whole body.

Yoga and dance are often movement meditations. In general, the idea is for the movement to be simple enough that it requires little thought, so you can let go into the experience, release the mind, and quiet restless thoughts.

Rhythm: There is a small amount of scientific evidence that rhythm has an effect on neurological function and can be healing. This evidence is growing as more scientists become interested in studying what mystics have known for millennia. It seems that rhythm can induce mental states that calm the mind, reduce mental "noise," and improve focus.

Drumming or light percussion (rattles, bells, finger cymbals, etc.) can be a powerful meditative aid. In fact, lots of people get hooked on drumming to the point where it becomes their primary or only ritual or meditative technique. For meditation purposes, a drum rhythm should generally be simple—you're going for a mild trance, not musical excellence.

Other rhythmic arts also have a meditative effect. Various textile crafts—stitching, weaving, braiding, knitting, and so on—can be used as meditation aids. They are silent but have the same repeated rhythm and physical focus as drumming, and can have a similar effect.

Sample Meditation Exercises

When I was first studying Wicca, my teacher gave me a sheet with some meditation exercises from *What Witches Do: The Modern Coven Revealed* by Stewart Farrar. First published in 1971, this book is an insider's look at the training system of a Wiccan coven—an important early work that is still relevant. Training materials in the occult being in short supply in those days, my teacher had copied the exercises and created a handout for students. The exercises were a great starting point for mind training. The first two meditation exercises that follow are drawn from that handout.

Exercise 4: Beginning Meditation #1

Begin by preparing yourself and your space for meditation, as described in the "Preparing to Meditate" section earlier in this chapter. Make sure you have the ability to relax and pay attention to what you're doing.

In a comfortable position, take several deep breaths, noticing yourself becoming relaxed and observant. Allow ideas and images to pass through your mind. Allow one idea or image to emerge, and begin to meditate on it.

For example, if you find yourself thinking of a tree…, picture a tree, analyse it, visualize its metabolism, its development, its life-span, its seasonal rhythm, its relation to its surroundings, … and instantly banish any 'non-tree' thought that starts to arise. … Keep this up for five min-

*utes on the first day, lengthening the exercise by one min-
ute a day until you reach ten minutes.*[6]

Exercise 5: Beginning Meditation #2

Once you're comfortable with the first exercise, choose
an image that you've used in that exercise, and this
time, focus not on a cluster of ideas or images but on

*a single thought or picture; statically, allowing neither
intrusion of other thoughts nor modification of the original thought. … Gradually increase the time until you can
manage a full ten minutes.*[7]

Grounding and Centering

Grounding and centering are a simple pair of mind skills that
bring you fully present within yourself (centering) and connect you to the earth (grounding). Most people use "grounding and centering" as a single phrase, but the techniques are
different, and despite the way the phrase is commonly said, I
prefer to center and then ground.

Centering

Centering should be a precursor to any other inner work,
ritual work, or magic. You should center as a first step before
beginning any meditation. (Ironically, a meditation practice
will improve your ability to center, so the two go hand in
hand.)

---

6. Stewart Farrar, *What Witches Do: The Modern Coven Revealed*
   (Custer, WA: Phoenix Publishing, 1989), 51.
7. Ibid.

To center:

- Begin with a deep, cleansing breath.
- Become aware of yourself: simply notice that you are present where you are.
- Locate the part of your body that feels like you. For many people, this is the solar plexus, or gut. For others, it's the heart or the head. Find that part of you—your center.
- Begin breathing in and out from your center. Feel your breath move to and from that spot.
- Notice there are parts of you that are not in your center. There are thoughts and concerns, hopes and ideas. Parts of you are in the past and the future, at work, with your family, etc. Gently bring everything back home to the center.

There are a number of visualizations that can accomplish centering. I like to picture my uncentered self as a flock of birds, and centering is bringing all the birds home to the nest. Others like to picture a large, diffuse aura growing tighter and closer to the body.

You can spend several minutes centering, but once you are practiced at it, it will take only a few breaths to be centered. This simple technique will enhance all your subsequent work.

Grounding

Grounding is done to connect you to a greater source of power than yourself and to anchor yourself. In the next chapter, we'll begin to explore raising power. One source of power we'll discuss is your own body. When raising power from the body, being grounded protects your health and well-being.

When performing healing magic, grounding protects you, allowing the healing to flow *through* you and the sickness to flow *away* from you without, in either case, subtracting from your own health. When I do healing magic as part of a ritual, I will ground and center at the beginning of the ritual and then ground again right before the healing.

When you're performing anything ritually or magically that takes you out of body—trance, astral travel, remote seeing, or the like—grounding keeps you connected to the physical and serves as a safety net, allowing you to easily return to your body and physical reality when needed. Even if you're not doing anything that intense, grounding helps if you're a person who feels a little woozy or out of it after ritual.

When I first started running a Wicca training group, I was not yet good at grounding myself. We would have one hell of a ritual, after which I would find myself asleep on the couch. I'd wake up and realize that my students had cleaned up after ritual for me while I was passed out. (I had *great* students.) Clearly, I needed better control of my energy! I concentrated on improving my grounding and conquered that particularly embarrassing problem.

There are probably dozens of methods to ground. One basic method is as follows:

- Begin with a deep, cleansing breath.
- Allow your (centered) energy to fill your body.
- Send an awareness of that energy down into the ground. If you are standing, send it through the soles of your feet. If you are seated, send it through the base of your spine.

- Connect your energy to the energy of the earth beneath you.
- Feel the energy of the earth coming back up and filling you, through the connection you have established.
- Sometimes I use a final step and send the energy out through the top of my head, creating a second energy exchange with the sky.

One common visualization for grounding is that of a tree. You imagine yourself to be a tree, rooted in the earth. The energy flowing down into the earth is your sap, and the return energy is the nourishment of soil and water. Connecting to the sky, if desired, can then connect you to the four elements as well—the fire of sunlight and the carbon monoxide/oxygen exchange of air correspond to and complement the earth and water of the soil.

In my book *The Elements of Ritual,* I use a grounding technique called "Pillars of the Temple," which is designed for a group. Each person envisions themselves as a pillar, connected at the base to the earth and reaching toward the sky. The group as a whole then visualizes itself as a circle of pillars, a place of worship. This is a visualization designed, not surprisingly, for a Wiccan worship circle.

Another visualization for grounding involves the chakras. While a typical chakra meditation involves rising up from the root chakra to the crown chakra, in order to ground, start at the crown chakra and move down, through the root chakra and into the earth. Then you can work your way back up again.

Another grounding method is to become aware of your body, piece by piece. Notice that you have toes. Notice that you have feet. Notice that you have ankles. Continue up through your body, to the top of your head. You can do this technique slowly, in minute detail, or very quickly.

The body-awareness technique has lots of variations, from visualizing light in each body part, one by one, to tensing and releasing each body part. All of these techniques bring you into your body, into the physical, and therefore into a connection to the earthy part of yourself.

Grounding and centering can be accomplished with breath and sound, moving from a slow, even breath, to a deeper breath directed toward your center, to a resonant toning that moves energy from your center and down into the earth, and then up again.

As with centering, grounding can be done slowly or quickly. For a beginner, I recommend starting slowly and really feeling each step. As you become used to the process, simply knowing you're going to do it will accomplish some of the work. A long, slow centering and then grounding can even be its own meditation session.

For an accomplished ritualist, the process can be completed in moments, as a preliminary step before magical work.

Merging

In group work, add a step that merges the group after grounding. (The step can easily be performed between centering and grounding as well.) This helps the group be fully together, united in purpose and energetically. You'll notice that in the "Pillars of the Temple" technique, I described each individual person as a pillar, and the group as a whole becomes a temple. Similarly, in a tree meditation, the group can become a grove of trees. There need not be an elaborate visualization. You can simply extend the awareness of yourself to encompass the group, understanding that you are all present for a shared purpose.

Visualization and Sensory Exercises

Visualization is the third essential mind skill for magic, but "visualization" is a misnomer. About 80 percent of people imagine and process information visually—they "picture" things in their "mind's eye." But 20 percent is a very large minority of people who are excluded by the phrase.

The grounding and centering steps in the previous section gave visualizations—picture yourself as a tree, picture yourself full of light, and so on. But for you, it may not be visual, or there may be visual components but it may not be *primarily* visual.

Any of the senses may be a part of your imagination. You may hear, smell, or taste in your mind's eye, or you may have a cognitive imagination—you just *know*.

I happen to be pretty weak visually. I see images sometimes, but my strongest sense-imagery is body sensation, and picturing words. So if you say "water," I might *see* "WATER" spelled out in my mind's eye, while I *feel* water: I become aware of the saliva in my mouth, the fluid in my eyes, and so on. A meditation practice and years of experience have allowed me to become familiar with how I imagine, and what does and does not work for me, so that I no longer think of myself as an imaginative failure—I'm just different.

Visualization and sensory exercises give you a chance to explore exactly what images your mind is best at using, while developing strong imaginative skills. In magic, you must "picture" (whether visually or otherwise) your target or goal, so these skills are essential. Just as exercise at the gym makes your body stronger, these exercises will make your ability to create imaginative imagery stronger.

Perform these exercises with the same preparation you give to meditation—have privacy, have time, and be comfortable.

Exercise 6: Mind's Eye

1. Close your eyes.

2. Center yourself.

3. Imagine a rose. See it clearly in your mind. Imagine the nuances of the color and its exact shade.

4. Picture the texture of the petals, soft, as if you are rubbing them between your fingers.

5. Inhale and experience the scent of the rose.

6. Imagine touching the thorns, and feel the prick of pain.

7. Turn the rose around so that you see it from all sides.

8. Let the image fade slowly before opening your eyes.

This exercise can be repeated with any number of items that can be seen and touched and can inspire other senses. Imagine foil and hear it crinkle. Imagine a barbeque and feel the heat waves coming off it. Continue to repeat this exercise regularly until you feel you can reliably create an image (or a sensory experience) as needed.

The Mind's Eye exercise places the image in your mind. The next task is to take the image out of your mind and place it before you. In other words, stop *acting like* you can see the image and actually see (and feel, taste, smell) it.

Exercise 7: The Apple

The Spiral Dance by Starhawk is the seminal work on its particular style of Witchcraft—freeform, intuitive, and politically conscious. If you came into the practice of Witchcraft any time between 1979 and 1990, you are virtually guaranteed to have read it. *The Spiral Dance* remains an excellent and essential book on the practice of Witchcraft. The following exercise comes from its pages. I could give you my own version of it, but this one is excellent and cannot be improved upon. Starhawk's book doesn't say if this exercise should be done with eyes open or closed. I recommend you close your eyes. As always, begin by centering yourself.

Visualize an apple. Hold it in your hands; turn it around; feel it. Feel the shape, the size, the weight, the texture. Notice the color, the reflection of light on its skin. Bring it up to your nose and smell it. Bite into it, taste it; hear the crunch as your teeth sink in. Eat the apple; feel it slide down your throat. See it grow smaller. When you have eaten it down to the core, let it disappear.

Repeat with other foods. Ice cream cones are also ex-cellent subjects.[8]

This exercise places the image directly before you. You are holding the apple, not imagining that you hold it. See it in your hand, not in a hand that you picture in your mind.

Exercise 8: A Circle

In Wicca and many other magical traditions, a circle is created as ritual space. The circle, a universal symbol of wholeness and infinity (as well as a bunch of other things), is used in many different ritual traditions, and, as discussed in chapter 3, ritual space offers advantages to the magician. So our next exercise will take the visualization skills you're learning and apply them to this practical end.

In exercise 6, the imagery was in your mind's eye. In exercise 7, you transcended that, and placed the image before you; the apple was in your actual hand, and you swallowed it down your actual throat.

In this exercise, you're going to keep your eyes open and visualize/sense on top of what you see.

1. Stand in a space you will use for magic. Hold a wand or athame (ritual knife) if you have one.
2. Center yourself.

8. Starhawk, *The Spiral Dance: A Rebirth of the Ancient Religion of the Great Goddess* (San Francisco, CA: Harper & Row, 1979), 50.

3. Starting in the east,[9] point your magical tool (or your index finger) toward the ground.

4. Moving clockwise, slowly draw a circle around yourself.

5. As you do so, picture a bright blue electric light coming from the tip of your magical tool/finger and reaching the floor.

6. Hear the crackling, electric sound of the light.

7. Smell the ozone-like burning.

8. Feel tingling in your hands.

9. See the blue coming from your tool/finger and, as it reaches the floor, remaining there, so that when you're done, you're standing in the center of a circle of blue crackling light.

10. When you've circled all the way around and you're back in the east, draw the light back into your tool or finger—the circle remains on the floor.

11. Hold the image of the circle.

12. Now return to the east and draw the circle back up into your tool/finger, again moving around clockwise.

13. When the circle is fully lifted, allow all sensations to return to normal. Your skin isn't tingling. There is no electrical odor or sound.

14. Take a deep breath and release it. You're finished.

---

9. I have a compass app on my phone—it's invaluable!

The three exercises in this section will help you develop sensory ability in your mind's eye, in your ability to imagine the "real" with eyes closed, and, finally, in your ability to imagine the real with eyes open, while actually doing something. As you become skilled at these, you will find that working magic becomes easier and easier. In addition, these exercises will familiarize you with your own imaginative strengths and weaknesses. Did light sparkle and crackle but have no odor? Practice your olfactory imagination, but also know that scent may not be your strength.

Using Triggers

You and I are no different than Pavlov's dogs. We respond to conditioning, and, because we are intelligent, we can use that to our advantage.

There are many things traditionally associated with magic, including:

- Incense
- Candlelight
- Magical robes and jewelry
- Magical tools (wand, blade, staff, etc.)

We're going to talk about these things later in detail—what they mean, why they work, and so on. For now, though, let's talk about how their use can enhance your ability to alter your state of consciousness.

The mind responds quickly to repetitive stimuli. Play the same music every time you meditate and you'll find that after a while, simply turning on the music will begin to place you in a meditative state. So *use* that knowledge, and select music that works for you.

The same is true for incense. I always burn incense when I meditate, and so, when I smell it burning, I am already starting my journey away from ordinary consciousness.

The same is true for anything on this list. A magical ring or bracelet that is worn only when magical work, meditation, or mind exercises are being done can become a trigger that is effective and reliable.

I was raised in a Jewish family, so I had no traditional association in my mind with incense until I started practicing Wicca. When I was about twenty-two, a boyfriend's close relative died, and I experienced Catholic church for the first time when I attended the funeral. The entire situation was very tense—in addition to the normal sorrow associated with a funeral, family secrets had come out while this relative was on his death bed, and everyone was on pins and needles.

Suddenly I was calm and relaxed. After a few minutes, I realized it was the church incense—the same Three Kings blend the High Priestess of my coven favored. The scent soothed and opened me even without my realizing it.

You may want to set a particular incense aside that means "magic" and/or one that means "meditation." That way, you can use other incenses for other purposes, which we'll discuss in the next chapter. I've seen ritualists swap out one incense for another for a spell, or create a blend.

As an example, suppose your go-to incense for altering consciousness is myrrh. If you choose to burn rose—for a love spell, say—you can start your ritual with myrrh and then switch to rose, or you can create a rose and myrrh blend especially for the occasion and burn it throughout.

Scent is an especially powerful inductive influence, but the same principle applies to music, garb, or a recited phrase.

Using Focal Objects

A focal object is something—a physical object—that you focus on when meditating, when doing divination, when practicing other mind skills—trance, visualization, active imagination, or astral travel, to name a few—or when doing magic.

When talking about meditation earlier in this chapter, we defined "inward" and "outward" forms of meditation—concentrating the focus *in*, onto the subject of meditation, or *out*, pushing the mind out and away. Focal objects have the same two possible effects.

Focal Objects to Draw the Attention In

- Idols or religious icons
- Tarot cards
- Astrological charts
- Tree of Life
- Photographs
- Mementos
- Written text—a prayer, koan, or affirmation, for example.

With these, and similar objects, you are focusing your attention and thoughts on what they are, what they represent, what feelings and thoughts they create within you, what wisdom they have to offer, or what memories or imagery they inspire.

Focal Objects to Push the Mind Out
- Candles and other sources of fire
- Crystals
- A black mirror
- A bowl of water
- Clouds

These types of objects allow you to "space out." We've almost all had the experience of gazing into a fire and finding ourselves lost. This whole category of focal objects helps engender that experience.

Some people are exceptionally good at mind skills that require tuning out from the conscious mind in this way. Scrying, for example, is gazing into a crystal, mirror, or water and allowing the eyes to unfocus, seeing peripheral images or visions. Other people are better at focusing in and find that visions arise only when the mind is *busy*, as in studying a tarot card or tracing a path along the Tree of Life.

In chapter 2, we talked about sympathetic objects. A sympathetic object can serve double duty as a focal object, allowing you to form a magical connection while at the same time focusing the mind.

A focal object can also be a source of power. In the next chapter, we'll dive into raising power, and discover what sorts of objects can help to raise power. Objects such as crystals can be sources of power as well as focal objects, again serving a dual purpose.

five

Raising Power, Part One:
Power Sources, Deity, and Self

In chapter 1, we said the things that make magic work are as follows:

1. Interconnection

2. Transcending space and time

3. Intention

4. Power

Having covered the first three, it's time at last to talk about power.

Where Does Power Come From?

Raising power is going to involve, first, figuring out where power comes from. It's so much easier to draw water if you know where the well is. For each source of power, we can then discuss how to access power from that source.

Power comes from:

- Deity (God, the gods, the Goddess, or however you prefer to identify deity)
- The self—mind, body, and spirit
- Natural sources
- Supernatural sources
- Power saved, accumulated, or stored in something
- Words of power

Power raised for magical purposes is generally not raised from only one of these sources. A ritual can and often does draw upon every power source listed here.

Power from Deity

One of the things that I hear practitioners of magic say quite often is that magic is pretty much the same thing as prayer. I've said it myself—magic is prayer with more "tech." In prayer, at least in the more famous religions of the world (I have gone on to say), you just pray, without worrying if your technique is effective. God is supposed to handle that part.

But is that true? Is magic really just prayer?

Magic and prayer are somewhat similar in that both have a goal that may be theurgic or thaumaturgic, and both access a source of power to achieve that goal. But there the similarity ends. (You might argue that all prayer is inherently theurgic—about God or the gods—but if you're praying for something specific to happen, like an illness to be healed or the Mets to win the World Series, then that's more like thaumaturgy, even if God is involved.)

Magic differs from prayer in that prayer acknowledges only one source of power—the entity to whom you pray—whereas I've offered a whole list of sources. Magic also differs in that you, the magician, are directing the outcome, whereas in prayer, at least in theory, you're supposed to let the gods decide what happens next, and humbly accept that outcome.

Magic is not, then, just prayer. What about the reverse? Is prayer just a form of magic, raising a particular kind of power in order to achieve goals? Again, I'd say no. Prayer does many of the same things as magic, just as it does many of the same things as meditation, but it primarily involves a *relationship*. You pray in order to form a connection with deity, and internally, in that relationship, you exchange energy, some of which can be used to achieve goals.

But what if you don't pray? In the introduction, I said your magic could be sacred or secular. If you are an entirely secular person and consider magic to be fundamentally atheistic, where does that leave you?

Simply, power from deity isn't a source you'll want to access. There are plenty of other sources of power available to you, so it's not a concern. You can skip the following section on accessing power from deity if it's uncomfortable for you, or you can read it purely academically.

Accessing Power from Deity

For every source of power, there are numerous ways to access that power. In each section, I've tried to be fairly exhaustive, although I'm sure the creative magical practitioner can find even more. Here, then, are some ways to access power from deity.

Prayer

One of the primary ways to access power from deity is through prayer. Prayer, as I've just said, is rooted in a relationship. Your prayer should be consistent with your relationship with the deity to whom you pray. If you don't believe in God, praying to God is not going to work. If you have a relationship with a deity based on your humility and accepting whatever Fate brings you, then asking for power to direct your fate in some way is inappropriate.

Prayer to a deity should also be consistent with the nature of that deity. Praying to Aphrodite for love is a good idea, but praying to her for stability, less so. If you have a conflict and pray to a god of war for a solution, don't expect peacemaking.

In other words, the relationship, and the request, should be respectful. Make no mistake—prayer is a request. Certain cultures, and certain deities, allow for a much more forceful energy exchange—the petitioner can be seen almost to threaten or make demands of the deity. An example is found in the worship of Kwan Yin, the Buddhist goddess of mercy. There is a traditional style of Kwan Yin statue with a removable hand. You can, in the course of petitioning Kwan Yin for what you want, remove her hand, hiding it until your wish is granted. Most Westerners would not consider this kind of blackmail to be a decent way to interact with a deity, as monotheistic prayer tends more toward the groveling end of the spectrum. Nonetheless, a prayer or petition is a request—you're asking for help, whether gently or forcefully, whether humbly or arrogantly.

Magic can be monotheistic, polytheistic, or atheistic, but a magical view of deity tends to see the deity as a component of the magic and to use to the deity almost as a magical tool. What is that deity's energy? What is that deity's particular strength? It's almost like you "use" Sarasvati to improve your studies, or Brigid for healing, or Hermes for safe travel. Considering how to utilize a deity in this way can be appropriate, but it can also be disrespectful. It's important to consider what the deity's will is in the matter, as well as your own will, just as you must consider the desires of the other members of a group if you do magic in a group.

Evocation/Invocation

While prayer or petition is the most common method of connecting to deities and therefore gaining power from them, evocation (or invocation) is also a means of raising power.

Consider prayer. You are talking to a deity—Gaia, for example—based on the assumption that she's there and she's listening. Perhaps you pause before you begin, and make conscious contact with her. Perhaps you even begin your prayer by asking her to be present and listen. Right there, that's the beginning of evocation.

But the magical/ritual act of evocation (or invocation) is much more elaborate.

In the occult, the distinction is made between *invoking* and *evoking*. To *invoke* is to summon a deity into your own body (possession, channeling, or "aspecting"), or into the body of another person, or sometimes into an object (generally an idol). To *evoke* is to summon the deity externally, asking the deity to be present in your ritual space but external to anyone or anything. Here, we'll deal only with evocation. Invocation is a much more complicated, advanced, and potentially risky endeavor, and whole books are devoted to the subject.[10] In truth, though, the part we're going to talk about is pretty much the same in either case. Invocation and evocation both involve raising and sending power, and it is in the sending that they become different. Here, we're talking about raising power.

Evocation and invocation raise power by bringing the deity present. The energy is *exchanged*; you almost can't help sending power to the deity as you call. The energy is then reciprocated and redoubled, the deity bringing much more energy than you sent. As this energy exchange occurs, one of two things happens. Either you succeed in bringing the deity present to your ritual and then receive energy from the deity for the rest of the work you do (thus effectively raising power from the deity for that work), or you continue to send back as you receive, back and forth, but now you are directing the energy toward the *invocation*.

Over the years, I have been part of many rituals that contained rather lackluster evocations. For this reason, it's worth going over the components of an effective evocation/invocation:

---

10. For example, Kenaz Filan and Raven Kaldera, *Drawing Down the Spirits* (Rochester, VT: Destiny Books, 2009).

1. Invitation or summons
2. Specificity in words and atmosphere
3. Descriptiveness
4. Praise
5. Need or reason
6. Greeting and/or thanks

Invitation or Summons: It is important to specifically ask the deity to be present, or call to the deity.

Specificity in Words and Atmosphere: This involves a number of things. First, with a deity with a very long history and many qualities, be specific about who you are calling: Kali, merciful mother, or Kali, devourer of demons? Oya, keeper of the gates of the cemetery, or Oya, winds of change?

I am not a fan of invoking a generic deity, but you may be invoking someone whose name is unknown to you (such as a Paleolithic deity or perhaps a being from a dream). In that case, you'll rely more heavily on descriptiveness, but use whatever *titles* you know.

Second, specificity means that your nonverbal call should be specific as well. When I speak with Kali, I rely on my Ravi Shankar recordings and burning sandalwood to create an atmosphere specifically evocative of her. Music, scent, color, and other components of your ritual setting can aid in making your evocation specific to the being evoked.

Descriptiveness: Partly, the purpose of being very descriptive is to key your own mind into what you're doing and to create atmosphere. Partly, it augments specificity: not just Kali, but many-armed Kali, not just Thor, but bearded and mighty, goat-rider and hammer-wielder. Partly, descriptiveness is one of the things that raises power. We'll get to the magic of words in the pages ahead, but I think you can already feel the way flowing and evocative words create an energy when you speak and listen to them. Finally, descriptiveness bleeds into praise. When you are detailed about the deity, the deity is more responsive, and this may be because the deity is being treated with respect.

We've all gotten form letters in the mail. "Dear Sir/ Madam" never makes us feel special. We've all also gotten email or snail mail in which our name is in the right spot, yet the invitation itself is still generic. A detailed, specific, and descriptive invitation makes someone (whether that "one" is human or deity) feel singled out and genuinely invited.

Praise: This is just polite. And practical. I assume that Gaia has more than one invitation tonight, so make sure yours gets her attention.

Need or Reason: An evocation should include the reason you are invoking the deity. In the case of raising power, you have a fairly specific magical purpose, although "so that I may worship you" is perfectly acceptable.

Again, consider the analogy to a human invitation. It's much easier to accept an invitation if you know what you're being invited to and why.

Greeting and/or Thanks: If you've ever taken any kind of sales classes or even studied how to do well at job interviews, you've heard the phrase "assumption of success." You assume the answer is yes and behave accordingly. That means you leave the interview saying, "I look forward to working together," not "I hope you like me!" An invocation or evocation should contain that assumption of success, and therefore it should end with a greeting. In other words, if your evocation worked, there's a deity present. *Say hello.*

Sample Evocation

Gaia, Lady of the earth, ground upon whom I walk, join me here!

You whose body is the very globe, you who mother all living creatures, you who nurture and hold us, join me here!

Bring your kindness and graciousness, your love and your stability, O glorious one.

With love I call, that you may lend power to my work.

Join me here!

Welcome, and blessed be.

Exercise 9: Evocation

Create an evocation to the deity or being (angel, nature spirit, etc.) of your choice. Be sure to include the following components:

1. An invitation or summons
2. Specificity in words and atmosphere
3. Descriptiveness
4. Praise
5. Need or reason
6. Greeting and/or thanks

Note that in order for your evocation to be specific and descriptive, you have to know something about the deity. Don't be afraid of research! And don't just use the first source you find, either. Use multiple sources to make sure you really understand the historical or mythological material. This does honor to the deity and improves your evocation.

For the purpose of this exercise, "that I may worship you" is sufficient need/reason. After writing the evocation, find a time to use it. Ground and center, then evoke. How did it feel? Did it bring you closer to the deity you evoked? What would you change?

Offering

As with evocation, making offerings raises power by exchanging power. You give to the deity, and power is released into the ritual space as a result.

Offerings can be specific to the deity as well. A little research will tell you that Hermes likes frankincense, honeycombs, and wheat, while Ganesha likes milk and sweets. Be sure that your research includes any potential offerings that are not acceptable—for example, Demeter is offended by wine.

Offerings can be from yourself. They can be offerings of creativity, performance, or artistry. You can sing, dance, recite, or play music as an offering.

Worship

Worship is a huge subject. It's a book in and of itself. I am treating it only briefly here. I'm addressing it for a few reasons: to be complete about power, and sources of power, as well as to analyze the whole idea of the relationship between magic and prayer, and get at some common falsehoods about that relationship.

If you were focusing your magical energy on a worship ritual or on theurgy, it would make sense to do all three of these things: evocation/invocation, offering, and prayer or petition. In that case, you would do them in exactly that order: First invite and greet, then, immediately after greeting, make an offering—again, it's only polite. Only after giving do you then ask to receive (petition).

Power from the Self

The primary source of power to be raised, most of the time, for most people, is from the self. This is really interesting when we contrast it with power raising in most works of fiction, by the way. The self is the source that almost all fiction leaves out. We're going to discuss other sources of power, and many of those are mainstays of pop culture: magic words, powerful objects, and so on. But, because pop culture ignores the self, or treats the self as "special" (some people are born to do magic, others are not), many practitioners are lacking in important information about the relationship between self and magic.

In the section on mind skills in chapter 4, I talked about the necessity to ground whenever you're pouring your self into magic, and now I'm saying that your self is *almost always* poured into magic. This should give you a hint! On the rare occasions when pop culture actually takes power-from-self seriously, it tends to get it kind of right, albeit over-dramatically. People *do* become exhausted, disoriented, or dizzy from raising power while ungrounded, and long-term it can affect your physical, mental, and spiritual health. If you are uncertain of your ability to ground yourself, then continue working on the exercises in chapter 4 before proceeding!

Raising power from the self can refer to a number of different things: You can raise power from your body, and many power-raising techniques are based in the body. You can raise power purely from the mind. You can raise power through emotions—technically, that's also the mind, or at least the brain, but in the occult we tend to classify mind and heart as different things. Finally, you can raise power from the spirit. This is so closely intertwined with raising power from the gods—the line between higher self and deity being kind of blurry—that I won't treat it separately in this section.

Accessing Power from the Mind and Heart

Power can be raised entirely from the mind, although most practitioners use a combination of mind and body, or mind and objects, or all three. Fiction abounds with sorcerers who furrow their brows and perhaps put a hand to their forehead, and create great magic that way. Most of us in the real world will benefit from using specific mind techniques while also employing other power-raising techniques. Most of us will also benefit from using something to help us concentrate and focus the mind, whether a candle we gaze at, or body movement, or what have you.

Remember that two of the things that make magic work are that we have focused intention and that we imbue our magic with power. The essence of "mind magic" is that we concentrate our focused intention, building the intensity more and more, until the power has reached the desired peak.

Meditation was discussed previously as a means to develop the ability to concentrate intention. It can also be used as a means of raising power: This time, though, you are meditating on your specific goal, focusing the mind clearly and intensely, pushing the thoughts toward the target.

This is where the heart comes in. Building thoughts to an intense pitch is often augmented by whipping up the emotions.

In the previous chapter, I talked about how intense emotion can both help and hinder a clear intention. You may have to temper your feelings, calm them, or set them aside while deciding to do magic and while preparing magic. But once you're here, ready to raise power, bring feelings in. While you *think about* your goal, also *desire* it. Long for it. Develop an unshakable passion for it.

Many people say that magic cannot work without strong emotion, that it is the key to a successful spell. I don't think this is true. Emotion is one source of power. There are many others. Not everyone has the same ability to access emotion in a cohesive and meaningful way, so that it can be directed on command. Some people who find expressing emotion awkward *socially* may have the same awkwardness when it comes to forming emotion *magically*—even though they feel deeply.

It's also true that you will sometimes raise power for a goal you are not personally passionate about. When I am doing magic on behalf of another person, there are times when I simply don't feel as deeply as the subject himself feels. So if Joe needs a job, Joe really, really feels it. Most books on magic will tell you that in the moment you do the spell, you must feel it deeply and want it more than anything in the world.

But it may be that the language of emotion doesn't accurately reflect how you approach that spell. If you concentrate your mind fully and completely, if your focus and intention are there, if you have *firm desire*, it may be that you don't experience that *emotionally* so much as *mentally*. That's okay. Joe's job, to you, is a little bit abstract—you're not the one at home sending out résumé after résumé—and so the emotional part may not resonate as perfectly.

Another method of accessing power through the mind is through trance and other deeply altered states of consciousness. Deeper trance states can allow you to take in power from sources not accessible to the ordinary mind, and power can be *sent* from such states as well.

Accessing Power from the Body

The human body is continually generating a variety of energies that can be considered "magical." This doesn't just occur during magic. The existence of these energies can only partially be explained because, in a scientific sense, there's barely any understanding of what magical power actually is. How is it different from ordinary energy? From an endorphin rush? From adrenaline-fueled intensity? From arousal? It's not particularly clear. We know that *all* of these things can be tapped for magic and can contribute to magic. What we don't know is if there's a dividing line between these physical/mental conditions that are partially or entirely understood by science, and the supernatural. For now, though, let's proceed with describing ways to access power from the body, and leave the science aside.

Movement, even the simplest movement, generates energy from the body. Indeed, many "Witch's dances" are little more than running around a circle. This may sound stupid at first, but it's effective and can be quite powerful, and has the advantage of leveling the playing field—the graceful and the graceless are equally gifted.

The technique of such a Witch's dance is simple: A group starts by standing in a circle and begins to walk slowly clockwise, perhaps with hands joined, perhaps holding up their athames or another ritual tool, perhaps in the classic "As above, so below" stance of the Magician from the tarot (figure 1). The group may do an incantation, or they may sing, or one person may sit out of the dance to play a drum or another instrument, or perhaps there is recorded music.

Gradually, intensity builds. Perhaps the tempo of the drum or music increases, or perhaps the chant or incantation grows faster, louder, more intense. The walk gets faster and becomes a run. Ultimately, hands are dropped, magic posture is no longer possible, and the group is running as fast as they can in the small circle, probably shouting and whooping as they do.

A running technique is best used by the able-bodied. A Witch I knew told me her group—older and with mobility issues—found that gently swaying back and forth while standing in place was surprisingly effective at raising power.

Figure 1: Magician Card:
"As Above, So Below"

Dance is also an effective way to access power from the body. I like to make a distinction between ecstatic dance and trance dance. Ecstatic dance is body-centered. It's often attractive to look at, as the dancer is expressing himself through dance and is letting go into an experience of the body moving, flowing with energy, creating energy, and interacting with energy. Steps are generally improvised and varied. Trance dance, by contrast, is often simple—a few repeated steps. Although trance dance can often look to the outside observer like not much is going on, the inner experience of the trance dance transports the mind into a deeper state of consciousness. The simplicity and low effort of the steps allows such a dance to be maintained over long periods, during which time can seem to slow or stretch.

The two types of dance are actually descriptive of two ways in which power can be raised from the body: intensely or gently. Whether running or swaying, ecstatic dance or slow, trance dance, power can be raised by pushing the body hard or by simply using the body.

A third type of magical dance is a group dance of organized steps. A variety of folk dances can lay down patterns in the mind and body, generate power through movement, create group unity, and be aesthetically pleasing to boot—all of which can contribute to magic.

Exercise 10: Movement Power

Experiment with movement.

In a group or with a partner, try holding hands and dancing in a circle, using a simple walking step and gradually increasing in speed. Do you feel power increasing? Do you feel energized? Is it fun? (Fun is a *great* source of power when used right.)

Try other kinds of movement. What is swaying from side to side like? What are folk dance steps like? What are jumping jacks like?

Working alone, do the same experiments. You might find the same techniques work differently alone.

Exercise 11: The Grapevine Step

The grapevine is a simple folk dance step that is the basis for other, more complex folk dances. It takes longer to describe than to learn!

Stand facing forward.

1. Cross your right foot in front of your left so that you're stepping to the left.

2. Step left with your left foot.

3. Cross your right foot *behind* your left, again stepping left.

4. Step left with your left foot.

That's all there is to it! Across, left, behind, left. It's okay to sway your body with your right foot, so that you face left, forward, right, forward.

This is a great step to use in a group because everyone can learn it in about three minutes. It's also a nice way of dancing alone. If you're raising power alone and feel self-conscious, a few organized steps can make it go more smoothly.

Working with intensity can be exhilarating, and it is certainly powerful. The complexity comes in sending power raised this way. How do you focus? How do you remember what to send, and where? We'll talk about this in the next chapter.

One intense way to raise power from the body is through sex. **Sex magic** has lots of advantages: it's enjoyable, it's accessible to most people, and it generates energy in an easily understood way. Sex magic can be done with any number of people. You can raise power from your body alone, with a partner, or in a group. Your own sexual preferences are your only limitations. Don't do anything sexually for magic that would make you uncomfortable if magic wasn't involved, and especially, don't allow yourself to be persuaded to do something that makes you uncomfortable for the sake of magic.

One of the beautiful things about sex magic is that sex may be the place where you first understood the transcendent power of the mind and body—even before you learned about magic. In sex, we can send our consciousness soaring, we can transcend ordinary space and time, and we can feel the immensity of the power of our own bodies—all without magic being involved. Now, this isn't everyone's experience of sex, but if it's yours, you'll probably feel a natural connection between sex and magical energy.

Physical **pleasure** raises power from the body, whether that pleasure is sexual or not. I once participated in a ritual in which power was raised from my body by being massaged. It felt great, it was a beautiful experience, and the energy was very real. Unlike sex, this really isn't something you can do alone!

Pain also raises a great deal of power. Many people would be loath to work with such a technique, for obvious reasons, but the power raised is very real. Working with pain doesn't mean doing anything that is inherently dangerous. The most common techniques are flogging (whipping with thick, flat straps that hit the body bluntly) or suspension.

Working with pain is also not something that should be done alone. It's not that you can't inflict pain on yourself; it's that you need someone monitoring you, protecting you, and, basically, managing you. At some point, you'll be "out of your mind"—and that's the goal. But out of your mind with pain poses a lot of risks—injury not least among them. You'll need help monitoring body temperature and hydration as well.

Neither sex magic nor pain magic should be done by people who have never experienced the non-magical version. There's a huge learning curve in both inflicting and experiencing pain safely. Even people who are sexual masochists—

who crave and desire pain—have to *learn how* to receive pain. Otherwise it's just *ow*.

The final source of power from the body that we're going to discuss is **aura work**. When I refer to the "aura," I mean the palpable field of energy that surrounds your body. In fact, "aura" refers to a number of layers of emanation surrounding any living creature—between seven and nine layers are usually described; some people include "physical body" as the lowest level. What I'm talking about here is the first level after the physical, usually called the "etheric body." It's about a half-inch to four inches of energy that tightly hugs the body, and it can be used to great effect in power raising.

The etheric body is considered to be a direct emanation from the physical body, which is why it's included here.

There are a number of power-raising techniques that use the etheric body. In fact, the first power I ever raised—quite accidentally—was done like this.

Hold your hands straight up, so the palms are flat and facing each other. Bring them slowly close together, without touching. Stop when you feel a cushion of energy between them—that's the etheric body. At first, it may feel almost imperceptible. Continue to move your hands in and out; as you do so, the energy field grows in size, and you become more adept at perceiving it. Experiment with hand movements that feel good and that help to grow the energy. Try forming a ball, or "pulling taffy," or rolling the hands one over the other. The ball (or other shape) of energy you create is ready for sending.

You can also do this technique with a partner or in a group, passing it back and forth or round and round. The first time I raised power this way, my girlfriend and I were playing a mime game, passing shapes back and forth. She made an ice cream cone, licked it, and passed it to me. I turned it into a hat, put it on my head, took it off, and handed it to her. She turned it into a tennis ball and served it, and so on. Soon we had a huge, warm, tingling wave of energy between our hands. This was the event that first got me researching magic—I had to know what to do with that energy!

I've used this technique with a group in a seated or standing circle as follows (figure 2): A slow drumbeat or a one-two count is needed to get you started. Bring your hands together (not touching) on one, and then on two, bring them out to the side so that you are almost touching your neighbors on either side. Then one, and your hands are together in front of you again, then two, and your hands are connecting (through the etheric body) to your neighbors.

Figure 2: Etheric Energy in a Group

The etheric body can also be used for a "touch" technique. Just as massage can be used to raise power through pleasure and physical sensation, you can massage the etheric body for pleasure, healing, and to use the etheric body (the physical body's nearest energy emanation) to move the physical body's energy.

Exercise 12: Etheric Body

Use the techniques just described to explore raising power with the etheric body. How close together do your hands have to be when you start the exercise in order for you to feel the etheric body? After you've been working with your hands for a while—several minutes at least—how far apart are they when you can feel it?

Work with a partner. Does the energy feel the same to both of you?

Exercise 13: Etheric Massage

Have your partner stand or sit comfortably with her eyes closed. "Massage" her without allowing your hands to touch her physical body. Do this for at least several minutes, massaging the etheric body and feeling the energy between your hands and her body.

Afterward, you can ask your partner to describe her experience. Did she feel the energy in the same spots that you massaged? Did it feel the same to both of you?

Accessing Power from the Mind and Body Jointly

I happen to think that the whole mind-body split is artificial. Every day, medical science is expanding its understanding of the mind-body connection, and I wonder if it's a "connection" at all; maybe it's more of a jumble. Maybe they're as separate as the oil and vinegar in your salad dressing—you can see the separation, but the taste is still a blend. Or maybe it's more like trying to separate the chocolate from the milk in chocolate milk—can't be done! All of the previous "body" power-raising techniques involved the mind; trance, ecstasy, being transported out of the self—these are all "mind" things.

Nonetheless, dance is still primarily physical and meditation is still primarily mental. In this section, we'll look at techniques that have specific components of both mind and body.

The first and arguably the most powerful of these is **rhythm**.

The use of rhythm has become increasingly prevalent in magical communities. When I first became involved with the Pagan and magical world in the 1980s, drummers were few and far between. Now they're everywhere. Drumming is powerful and accessible and has an immediate effect on those who experience it.

Drumming isn't typically thought of as a part of Western magic, although Gerald Gardner wrote about its power in *Witchcraft Today* and claimed the New Forest coven in England had preserved drumbeats that could affect the mind powerfully.[11] Nonetheless, most drumming came into Western magic from African, Afro-Caribbean, and Native American traditions. As these communities cross-pollinated more

---

11. Gerald Gardner, *Witchcraft Today*, 142.

in the 1990s, drumming became more prevalent at gatherings and the practice caught on.

Rhythm is not limited to drumming, although given drumming's popularity, many people seem to forget that! It's really great to have quieter rhythm techniques in your repertoire, especially if you have neighbors or housemates. These include quieter musical instruments: rattles, maracas, clave sticks, finger cymbals and other bells and cymbals, and more. Rhythm can also be made with the body—clapping, snapping fingers, stomping, and so on.

Clapping games, such as those played by schoolchildren, can be used for power raising. (The ones I remember from childhood include "Miss Mary Mack," "Miss Susie," and "One Potato, Two Potato,") If you've ever seen schoolchildren play those games, you know how much energy they generate!

Research on the effect of rhythm on the brain is happening now, and early results are intriguing. Recent studies suggest that rhythm can sync up parts of the brain, making them function more effectively. In fact, being out of sync seems to be related to diseases such as Alzheimer's, and listening to rhythmic music seems to promote healing, although the research is still nascent. One study suggests that groups listening to the same rhythm appear to sync up their very thoughts. Former Grateful Dead drummer and Rock and Roll Hall of Fame member Mickey Hart has been collaborating with scientists to understand rhythm's effect on cognition and mood.[12]

---

12. Natasha Geiling, "Former Grateful Dead Drummer Mickey Hart Composes Music from the Sounds of the Universe," *Smithsonian* (October 1, 2013), www.smithsonianmag.com/science-nature /former-grateful-dead-drummer-mickey-hart-composes-music -from-the-sounds-of-the-universe-265907.

What we know is that rhythm affects the brain, and that different rhythms have different effects—rhythms can variously make you calm, agitated, aroused, focused, and spaced out. By controlling your mood, transporting your consciousness, and rousing your spirit, rhythm raises power through the mind.

Rhythm also affects the body. Our bodies have a host of physical and neurological rhythms, and basic physical health depends on these internal rhythms. We breathe, sleep, wake, and walk in rhythm. Our life literally depends on the rhythmic beating of our hearts, and a heartbeat rhythm is incredibly powerful to use in ritual and magic. The body naturally sways to a good beat, and this does a lot of things: it helps raise power through movement, it lets the mind release as the body takes over, and, in a group, it creates unity as each body responds to the same beat, which also increases power. Rhythm and dance are closely related. Rhythmic sound helps the body groove when dancing and moving, and dance itself can be used to create a rhythm.

Playing a rhythm on an instrument, or with your body, or dancing a rhythm, or vocalizing a rhythm, can all be an important part of power raising, and all are easily accessible means of raising power.

Similar to rhythm is **repetition**. Repeated patterns soothe the mind. There's a vast amount of literature on the pleasure of repetition, and here, too, neuroscience is becoming quite interested. Repetition promotes learning. It is paradoxically both calming and stimulating. Large patterns of repetition (daily routines) and small patterns (tapping the fingers, doing the same thing over and over) have similar effects.

Repetition is used *all over the place* in magic. Obviously, a rhythm is an example of a repetition, and indeed, you can take one or more complex rhythms and repeat them, overlaying the two, or overlay one or more complex beats on top of a heartbeat. If you're a talented drummer or you have multiple drummers working together, you can ascribe different magical intentions to different beats. Suppose, for example, you are raising power for a healing. A simple, soothing beat can be used to calm and ease the patient, while a fiery tempo overlaid on top of it can represent the fire of the life force—both are needed for healing.

Repeated phrases within an incantation or evocation are hypnotic and effective. In the sample evocation to Gaia earlier in this chapter, the phrase "Join me here!" is repeated three times. When Lewis Carroll said, "What I tell you three times is true," he was on to something. The use of triple repetition is ancient in storytelling and proverbs as well as magic. When you repeat a phrase, it reinforces it in the mind, and it creates a resonance in the body.

Textile magic is something not often discussed in the occult. It's very ancient, although I confess I coined the phrase just now in order to discuss a group of techniques that raise power using a variety of textiles. The use of a spinning wheel, a loom, of knitting, stitching, weaving, and making knots, all have a long history in magic. They all rely on repetition and rhythm to create a trance state in the mind, while the repetitive movement in the hands (and sometimes feet, with a loom or spinning wheel) has its own impact. Later, we'll discuss using knots to "tie up" an intention. Here, we're concerned with the *act* of tying a knot or, more likely, a series of knots.

Think of how often you've heard of this kind of magic in folklore and myth! In Greek mythology, we have the three

Moirai (Fates), who spin, measure, and cut the thread of life. The goddess Athena is a master weaver, and Arachne, goddess of spiders, rivals Athena in weaving. Theseus escaped the labyrinth by following a thread.

In Norse and Germanic myth, Frigg is associated with weaving, and Holda with weaving and spinning. The Valkyries used looms strung with the bodies of their enemies.

In fairy tales, we have Sleeping Beauty. The spell that puts her to sleep was on the spindle of a spinning wheel. The Brothers Grimm tell the tale "Spindle, Shuttle, and Needle," in which a spinning spell brings a suitor to a girl.

Most textile magic is done alone, although knotting, braiding, tying, and shaping string or yarn can be done by a pair of people, as in a Cat's Cradle game. Stitching can be done in a group, and a quilting bee can be magical indeed.

Textile magic uses mind and body, and occasionally group unity. It lulls and hypnotizes with repetition while creating something and transforming something, and this is what gives it its great power.

Exercise 14: Knots

Learn how to make some simple knots with string. During meditation, make knots as a counting device—that is, use knots the way you might use mala beads or a rosary, to count repetitions of a prayer, mantra, or phrase.

Practicing knots will have magical application later, and practicing them during meditation will have a synergistic effect—your knot-making will become more powerful and your meditation will be deeper.

Music is another extraordinary way to access body and mind power together. Music, too, has healing properties that science is beginning to recognize, and is used increasingly in conventional therapies. Music seems to transcend ordinary ways of using the brain, and so can promote healing and learning. **Sound** creates vibration, which moves the body and causes a number of internal chemical reactions. When we chant and tone, we move vibration through the centers of our bodies. A deep "om" comes from the belly, up through the chest and through the throat, then fills the mouth and nose, and reverberates in the top of the head.

Chants, songs, intonation, and intoned sound affect the body, while the words being uttered in these songs (if any) engage the mind. As you raise power through your body in the act of chanting, and, if in a group, raise power through unity as well, a part of your mind is engaged with the meaning of simple lyrics. Because such words can have a profound impact in a magical context, I am careful about choosing chants for my work that are positive, forward-focused, and purposeful.

Sound doesn't have to be generated by the body to have an effect on the body. A Tibetan singing bowl is an example of an instrument that is played in order to affect body and mind, inducing relaxation and a meditative state. Vibration, resonance, meditation, relaxation, and trance are all related, and all can be generated or promoted by sound.

Austerities as a means of power raising refers to the whole class of techniques in which the body is subjected to extremes, either over a period of time or during meditation, or both. Mind power is accessed through trance and deep meditative states, while the body is the instrument through which extreme states are reached. As with using pain or sex as a part of magic, austerities are for advanced practitioners.

In Hinduism, extreme austerities, asceticism, and deprivation are used to produce *tapas*, an intense heat from the body that brings great power as a byproduct (because in Hinduism the goal is enlightenment, not power). Simple examples include fasting, isolation, and other ascetic practices.

A more extreme austerity is sensory deprivation, which includes isolation tanks (extremely pleasant to most people) and the use of the "Witch's cradle," which is a suspension basket or hammock—the practitioner is both isolated (in the "cradle") and suspended, and sometimes bound as well. Other forms of suspension are also used, and these include hanging upside down as well as combining suspension with pain (flogging, whipping, or piercing). To generate tapas, yogis will use extreme postures, such as standing on one foot for days. Bondage techniques can also be used, combined with isolation, with pain, or with posture, to produce an intense body-mind reaction.

Again, none of this is for the beginner or for anyone working alone!

Raising Power, Part Two:

Natural and Supernatural Sources, Accumulated Power, Magic Words, and Flavor

Let's continue our exploration of sources of magical power, starting with sources from nature and the supernatural.

Power from Natural and Supernatural Sources

As you may have gathered from reading this far, the dividing line between natural and supernatural is somewhere between fuzzy and invisible. That being the case, it makes sense to group these two power sources together, rather than wait until science settles the question(s).

Among natural sources, I include both the macro and the micro. Macro-nature is nature itself: mountains, oceans, caves, soil, forests, deserts, storms, rivers, and so on. The life force inherent in these may or may not be considered supernatural. Wights, devas, nymphs, fair folk, and other nature spirits are hard to separate from the nature they inhabit (*Am I raising power from a tree or from a dryad?*)—yet another reason this section includes both, jointly.

Accessing Power from Nature as a Whole

One way to raise **power from nature** is by calling upon it (or upon its spirits) and asking for it. Picture, for example, standing in the waves and saying something like this:

Beloved ocean, I stand here with you.
Mighty ocean, let your power wash over me with each wave.
Let your power fill me.
Beloved ocean, I stand here with you.
Make me buoyant with you.
Make me strong as you are strong.
Make me deep as you are deep.
Make me resilient as you are resilient.
Beloved ocean, I stand here with you
And ask for your power.
I thank you. Blessed be.

Note that I have used a triple repetition as well as an assumption of success. Evocation to call a nature spirit is pretty much the same as evocation to call upon deity, and the same principles apply.

Of course, you could just be out in nature, at some natural spot, and not say anything. Your call could be entirely mental or emotional, reaching your mind and spirit to the mind/spirit of the place and taking the power in. I'm a fan of verbalizing things, but you'd expect that from a writer, and that may not be your style. You could call through music, or through dance, or through whatever means feels right to you.

Another way to access nature's power is simply to do your magic outdoors, in nature. While raising power through other means, you are also connecting to this power. For example, drumming on the beach accesses the body-mind power of rhythm *and* the natural powers of the beach and ocean. The same could be said for sex magic in the woods or chanting in the desert. Combining techniques is almost always a part of magic. You can have sex *while* chanting in the woods, or drum *and* dance on the beach.

Exercise 15: Being in Nature

Figure out what macro-nature is accessible to you. Is there a beach nearby? A forest? Where can you find nature in your life? Even city dwellers should do this exercise. Maybe it's a park, or maybe it's roof access that allows you to be with the open sky.

Suburban life tends to offer little bits of nature, but if you live in the suburbs, see what wilder parts of nature are accessible to you.

Once you've found a natural spot, ground and center there. Reach out with your feelings, and see if you can sense the power of the nature around you. What does it feel like? Is it strong? Gentle? Loving? Wild? What is the power you are feeling?

Do you feel an affinity for this place? Does it feel like "your place"?

Leave a small offering to the spirits of the place when you go.

Exercise 16: Building an Inner Location

Many magicians use a meditation technique called "building an inner temple" (or a similar name—depends on who you ask). This is a long-term project done in a meditative state. The project is for someone already practiced at the basic mind skills explored in chapter 4. You should already be comfortable meditating and focusing.

Once you have the needed mind skills, you can undertake this project as a part of your meditation practice. You'll be devoting (approximately) twenty minute sessions to this project, and you'll be coming back to it regularly.

The steps are as follows:

1. In meditation, begin a journey to someplace special. Your task, in the beginning, is threefold. First, choose what purpose your "someplace" is for, what such a special place will mean to you. It could be a beach, a cave, a cottage in the woods, a castle, a garret, a treehouse—the possibilities are endless. Second, be open: When you arrive at your someplace, it may not be what you thought it would be. Don't force it—this is a process of discovery as much as creation. Third, pay attention to the route. You will be repeating this inner journey many times, so you should know the path/

road/stairs/highway/train … However you travel, it should be repeatable and reversible (in other words, you can go there again, and you can come back).

2. In subsequent meditation, return to this location. Now you are studying two things. First, you are studying the path. This should become second nature to you, and the project is not complete until you are confident that *this* path brings you to *this* place. Second, you are studying the location itself. Begin exploring it. Suppose, for example, you're in a cottage. Is there furniture? Are there drawers in the furniture? Open the drawers and see what's in them. Suppose you're at the beach. What color is the sand? Is it a seaweed-covered area, or a rocky area, or a sandy area? What is the shape of the shoreline? Over the course of multiple meditation journeys, your explorations can become more detailed and range farther afield, always keeping your "someplace" as the central touchstone location.

3. Once you are confident that this is a place you know, can return to, and *want* to return to, start bringing things on your journey. This means you will have to find a place to leave them there. In a cottage or castle, this may be simple, but on a beach or in the woods, you may need to find or build a natural or humanmade storage location, whether it's a hole in the ground, a hollow of a tree, a wooden box, a beach cabana, a lean-to, or

something more elaborate. (If you have chosen to take on a building project in your location, then that is an extra step prior to bringing things to leave there.) The things you bring depend, obviously, on the purpose of the location you've chosen. Let's assume you've created a location in which to raise power. In that case, you may wish to bring a wand or an athame, a drum or a flute, a magical robe, an incense burner, or whatever other magical tools feel appropriate. Perhaps you want firewood and a few books of matches. You'll probably want to return to the location and check on the things you've left, to feel confident they're there, and intact, before relying on them.

The practice of creating an inner location as described here has many uses. In this case, we're discussing it in the section on power from nature, because you can build a natural location that you can return to at times when visiting the physical location is not possible. This allows you to connect to nature and access nature's power even when you're stuck indoors for whatever reason.

Of course, such a natural location can also be soothing, renewing, and centering for you, and can be a refuge, above and beyond its power-raising advantages.

Understanding Nature

It helps, if you're accessing power from nature, to *understand* nature. This means understanding things like moon phases, growing seasons, solstices and equinoxes, and other seasonal, annual, monthly, and daily cycles. It helps to know a bit about your local weather patterns, plants, and animals. Ceremonial magicians pay attention to astronomical and astrological cycles as well—planetary hours, for example.

Witches especially work heavily by moon phase:

- The full moon is a time of power and rebirth. Often it is reserved for theurgy.
- The waning moon (from full to new) is a time of diminishment. Magic done at this time is to cause things to shrink or depart.
- The new moon is a time of darkness and mystery. Often it is reserved for meditation and shadow work or for divination.
- The waxing moon (from new to full) is a time of growth. Magic done at this time is to cause things to grow or come to fruition.

Solar cycles are variable, depending upon where you live. I'm from a temperate zone with four seasons—spring and summer are when I do outward-focused, community-building work, while fall and winter are introspective and a good time for solitary work. If you live in a tropical region, or a desert, or even in Northern California, with rain and drought cycles, your understanding of seasons will naturally differ.

Solar and agricultural cycles vary by region but also by tradition. Like many Wiccans, I follow the eight-spoked Wheel of the Year, but the meaning of those seasonal energies might not apply to the tradition you're working, or might not feel right to you, if you're not working a specific tradition.

Things like planetary hours, retrogrades, and moon voids require specialized reference materials both to know when they occur and to understand their import.

Accessing Power from Natural Things

The "things" I'm referring to in this heading include animal, vegetable, and mineral things—a virtual Twenty Questions of magic. Since they all exist in the physical world, we can agree they're natural, despite that fuzzy dividing line we've discussed.

The fuzziness in the case of most natural things has to do with how the power is accessed and the nature of that power.

Let's take lavender as an example. Lavender is a flower (vegetable, if you're still playing Twenty Questions) with relaxing and healing qualities. Lots of research supports the use of lavender for its calming and sedative effects.[13] Some of the related effects have less research supporting them (antidepressant and insomnia relief, for example), but research is growing. So if you were to inhale lavender oil, apply it topically, or even drink a lavender tea in order to relax, then everyone could agree that you would be using a natural power and accessing it in a natural way.

But suppose you were doing distance healing. You might be in Kansas, sending relaxing energy to someone in Seattle. In that case, would the use of lavender in your spell suddenly make the power supernatural instead of natural?

Let's start by understanding that natural substances have certain properties, and those properties can be accessed for

---

13. University of Maryland Medical Center, "Lavender," https://umm .edu/health/medical/altmed/herb/lavender.

magical purposes. Those properties might have non-magical application as well—such as lavender for relaxation—or they might not.

One of the things that's important about this notion of the powers of natural things is that it answers an age-old question about magic: Is it all just a placebo effect? Is it all in the mind? Certainly even well-known magicians have written that the most important aspect of magic is its effect on the mind of the practitioner, as well as the mind of the subject. It's also very "civilized" to look at the inexplicable—be it a death curse or a miraculous healing spell—and explain it away by saying "placebo effect!" But as long as there has been magic that has used the power of suggestion—and that's millennia, make no mistake—there have been magical brews, potions, and objects. Natural substances draw on a power from *outside* of the self. In this way, these substances expand your own power, and the potential of your magical work. It's also a different way of looking at magic and, I think, an important way.

Natural Substances Include:

- Herbs
- Plants
- Flowers
- Wood
- Mosses
- Fungi
- Other plants or plant parts
- Spring water, ocean water, and other naturally occurring liquids

- Stones, including meteor stones
- Crystals or gems
- Resins
- Bone
- Hair
- Blood
- Other bodily fluids
- Other animal parts

Kinds of Power That Can Be Accessed

Natural substances start with generally agreed-upon **natural qualities**, whether or not those qualities are well studied by science. Plant substances have chemical natures that affect the mind and body. Less agreed-upon but still based in the physical nature of the object is the molecular structure of crystals, the natural properties of magnets, and other mineral properties. Everything on the previous list has inherent natural properties that can be leveraged by a magician.

Sympathetic qualities are typically well known in folklore. The heavy, solid, cool sensation of holding a hematite, for example, lends people to use it for grounding. It *feels* grounding—so we can say it has sympathy with the sensation of grounding. Mandrake is a plant with folklore based on its appearance—it looks like a man, and its association with fertility comes from that.

How to Access Power from Natural Things

Natural and sympathetic qualities can be accessed **directly**— for example, drink the tea, hold the magnet, inhale the aroma. They can also be accessed sympathetically.

This may be confusing, because I've just said you can access a sympathetic quality sympathetically. But other than the weird sentence structure, it's actually pretty simple.

Access a quality through sympathetic magic by using it in a sympathetic way. For example, you could stuff a poppet (a magical doll) with rose petals to create love in the person represented by the doll. This is a form of imitative magic in which the doll—which has sympathy with the person it looks like—"behaves" as the actual person should—it receives the love. You could also rub a healing crystal on a photograph of a person being healed. The photo is the sympathetic object, and the patient is accessed sympathetically through it.

I keep a little protective mojo bag in my car. It has a variety of consecrated substances with safety, general protection, and anti-theft properties. It also has consecrated coffee beans to keep me alert behind the wheel. Here, we're using the natural property of caffeine in a sympathetic way—caffeine doesn't *naturally* work by simply being nearby.

Here's an example of the opposite: use of a sympathetic property in a direct way. Salt is a natural preservative—it prevents food from going bad. For this reason, it is associated by sympathy with purification. If I consecrated salt and then cooked with it, I would be directly ingesting the sympathetic quality of purification, as well as the natural quality of deliciousness.

Magical tools made from natural substances will partake of the natural and sympathetic powers of that substance, and when the tool is used, the power will be accessed.

To sum up, means of directly accessing natural power include:

- Eating or drinking (if safe)
- Inhaling
- Wearing
- Carrying
- Placing on the altar

Indirect (or sympathetic) access to natural power is, generally, connecting the substance to a sympathetic object (a photograph, a poppet, etc.).

Natural qualities are those inherent in the substance—coffee makes you alert, valerian makes you sleepy. Sympathetic qualities are apparent from the folklore and magical associations of a thing and generally are based on a similarity (connection) to the natural quality—salt purifies, snakeskin brings renewal, hematite is grounding.

It's not necessary to know where a thing's magical properties come from in order to use it. If you have reputable reference materials, go ahead and use them. For example, I often refer to *Cunningham's Encyclopedia of Magical Herbs.* Since Scott Cunningham was known as a thorough researcher, it's a trustworthy resource. I may not always know if the property of an herb, gem, or other natural object is inherent in the object (such as comfrey is good for broken bones), or directly sympathetic (such as salt's purification qualities), or symbolically sympathetic (amethyst is wine-colored and therefore associated with sobriety), or if it's associated with an old story, a social custom, astrology, or some lost bit of folklore. Some of this shades into our next section on accumulated power, but if the power is there, it doesn't really matter whether or not you can parse out exactly how it got there.

Elemental Power

The four elements are both natural and supernatural. They're natural in that they are rooted in nature—air is the sky, the wind, and the air we breathe. Fire is itself, fire, as well as heat in general. Water is all of the waters of nature, from oceans to ponds, as well as liquids generally, including bodily liquids—blood, sweat, and tears. Earth is soil, the ground generally, stone and stone formations—especially caves, which are both stone *and* in the ground—and minerals generally.

The occult understanding of the four elements is considerably more abstract, extrapolating out quite a distance from the simplicity of the naturally occurring elements. Using salt to represent earth is an example of a slight abstraction. Using feathers to represent air is more abstract—birds fly in the air, therefore feathers have a sympathetic connection to air. Lots and lots of things have sympathetic connections to the elements, and the appendices in this book provide tables, including a table of elemental correspondences and symbols. (Not everyone uses a fifth element—spirit. If you do, then representing this element is far *more* abstract, since you'll be using something physical to represent the quintessentially non-physical.)

In addition to having representations that are sometimes abstract, elements have a quality that transcends nature and so can be considered "supernatural." Around 450 BCE, the philosopher Empedocles theorized that the four elements were the roots of the cosmos. Most importantly, he said that the elements cannot exist in pure form in nature, but are always mixed and adulterated when in physical form. These ideas are highly influential within occult thought to this day. Consider water, for example. As found in nature, water has air bubbles (even if not carbonated), it has mineral content, and it has varying degrees of heat—all three of the other elements are present. Accessing an element, then, is using its natural form to access something *beyond* that form, to reach a spiritual or astral essence of that element and connect to it.

When looked at this way, we can easily understand why a magician might ritually purify the elements—this act brings the true, unadulterated form of the element to the rite. We can also understand how an element can be associated with a direction. Sitting at my desk, I know that air (the sky) and earth (the ground) are in every direction surrounding me, just as I know that the nearest body of water is about a mile due east. However, if we're talking about the pure, metaphysical elements as understood in the occult, we can understand each element as having an inherent nature that is specific and transcends local geography. Metaphysically, Western occultism places water in the west even if the Hudson River is just to your east.

Most of the time, elemental power is accessed in ritual by purifying the elements and having them present on the altar. They can then be used for additional purifications and/or consecrations, for example, by wetting an object in saltwater (water and earth) and passing it through incense smoke (air and fire), or by using each of the four elements separately.

Elemental power can also be accessed more directly. You can spend time in a very "airy" or "earthy" place and draw upon the needed power in such a place.

Objects consecrated to, or containing, one or more elements can be incorporated into other magical objects—embedded in a wand, sewn into a robe, stuffed into a poppet.

Natural substances and objects can serve a dual purpose. For example, suppose you were healing someone with a balance disorder. Earth might help ground and stabilize the person, so use a healing herb in your spell that is also associated with the element of earth.

Elements can be accessed through meditation or ritual invocation/evocation. If you are drawing the elements into your ritual space or into your person, you should first know them well through meditation. (My book *The Way of Four* has elemental meditations and exercises designed to increase your intimacy with the elements, and you may find it useful.)

Finally, elemental power can be accessed through the *beings* of the elements: elementals. Known as sylphs (air), salamanders (fire), undines (water), and gnomes (earth), the elementals are supernatural beings, usually noncorporeal, who are composed entirely of their own elements.

I want to emphasize here how very difficult elementals can be to understand, let alone control. You and I are made up of four elements. We have the intelligence of air, the willpower of fire, the emotionality of water, and the practicality of earth. We are so used to being complex and having all these powers are our fingertips that we often can't imagine what it's like to be so singular. If you invite a salamander into your home, it will light fires. It won't do this because it's malicious or destructive, but simply because it's *fiery*.

I speak from experience. I will never forget the Great Salamander Infestation of 1985. My roommate was allowing her young daughter to fry plantains, while she got drunk and passed out on the couch. The oil caught fire and then the kitchen curtains, then the fire department came, and by the time I got home from work that evening my former kitchen was a charred cavern with a hole that had been chopped in the ceiling by the good people of the FDNY. Along with cockroaches (we'd managed to conquer them in our apartment, but the hole gave them a reentry point), we ended up with an apartment full of salamanders.

It was little things, one after another, that alerted me to their presence. I was meditating in the bath, as is my habit, and the censer somehow fell over, spilling hot coals everywhere. Candles tipped over. I finally understood what was happening one night when I was lying on the couch reading and realized that I had been ripping up little strips of paper and setting them on fire in the ashtray. I hadn't been fully aware I was doing it, but one little strip ended up not being quite so little, and the fire flared up and startled me into wakefulness. That's the moment when I understood that salamanders were in the joint.

The infestation ended comically. I was young and new to magic, and spoke to my teacher for advice. I then *politely* ritually requested that the salamanders vacate the apartment. They left—taking the hot water with them for four days.

I like telling that story, and I've told it in print before, because it's funny and dramatic and completely true, and it also makes a point. Elementals are unpredictable. They are beings with their own inner nature, and they aren't easy to boss around. Calling upon them for elemental power is a practice best left to the experienced ritualist, and is best done in a magically contained space, such as a cast circle, so that they don't get out and start knocking over censers. Fortunately, there are many other ways to draw on elemental power.

Other Supernatural Beings

Discussing elementals naturally leads to a discussion of other noncorporeal entities, and there are lots of them. We've already covered deities and nature spirits as well as elementals. There are also angels, the Mighty Dead, daemons, demons, the fair folk, ascended masters, and so on.

There is no question that calling upon such beings can provide you with a great deal of power. But if elementals—smallish beings compared to angels, demons, or fairies—can cause so much trouble, imagine what calling upon larger powers can do! I've seen *Fantasia* and have no desire to reenact "The Sorcerer's Apprentice."

To be fair, most of the problems that magicians have with these kinds of entities are nothing like those in *Fantasia*. The fact is, angels and the like don't necessarily make strong connections to what you and I might call "the real world." They often don't care to make sure you eat, sleep, or hold a job. It's necessary to control what your relationship with these entities is like and what limitations are placed on it. If you are in communication with such entities, keep in mind that you have every right to establish your own boundaries and limitations, and those can be negotiated.

It also seems to be true that the dead and other non-physical beings operate at a higher vibrational frequency than we do. Unable to slow their own vibration down, they tend to speed ours up, which has metabolic repercussions. In short, it's not all that good for your health to be channeling or communicating with such entities on a regular basis. You have to pay a lot of attention to your body on your "off-hours," and make sure you *have* off-hours.

Because entire books are devoted to the subject of how to invoke such beings safely, effectively, and powerfully, I won't attempt to dig into the subject here. As with elementals, you need the ritual skills before you can start bringing other-worldly beings into ritual space. If you develop such skills and work appropriately, the experience can be rewarding and enriching. My own son works as a medium, so I'm not putting it down!

Ancestor Altars

There is an exception to the rule that you need a lot of ritual safety to call upon otherworldly beings—that is, calling upon your own Beloved Dead. Maintaining an ancestor altar is a way to connect to those you've loved who have left this world, and to pray for them to aid your magical work as well as your day-to-day life. A loving and respectful relationship with your ancestors can bring you protection, support, and energy.

A huge number of traditions have ancestor worship or veneration as part of their practice. From China to Hoodoo, from ancient Rome to modern Paganism, ancestor altars are widespread. Some of the details vary from tradition to tradition, but many of the basics are the same:

- A permanent altar honoring your beloved departed or your direct kin should be set up and well maintained. If you commit to this, that means it should be clean and cared for regularly. Since you're committing to the process of caring for the altar, think seriously about who should be on it—lots of ancestors means lots of work.

- "Ancestors" can mean those in your family who have passed on, whether you knew them or not. Some people have altars only for those they knew personally, and some go back generations. Some include non-relatives, either friends who've passed on or teachers, known to you or not. A Wiccan might have Gerald Gardner on her altar; a psychiatrist might have Sigmund Freud.

- Pictures and mementos of your dead can be placed on the altar, as well as funerary items (crematory ashes, for example). Something that was known to be a favorite of an ancestor can be included, and that can be anything from a shot glass, to a crossword puzzle, to a baseball.

- Offerings at the ancestor altar should be something your beloved dead would like—don't offer whiskey to someone who was in AA. Typical offerings are water, whiskey, candy, or flowers.

- After making an offering, simply commune with your ancestors. Allow them to let you know what offerings they'd like and how they want this relationship to go.

- If you feel the need to have a short break from the watchful eye of your ancestors or want some privacy, it's okay to cover the altar with a clean cloth for a bit.

Supernatural Things

Certain things are considered to have inherent supernatural qualities, just as certain things have inherent natural qualities. Many of the charts and correspondences that a magician uses will be for the purpose of accessing such supernatural qualities.

Numerology is an example: it accesses the inherent supernatural qualities of numbers. Of course, the thing about numerology is that it's culturally driven—there are various systems from various sources. We will cover cultural power in the "Saved, Accumulated, or Stored Power" section that follows. For now, it's best to understand that Pythagorean/Western, Kabbalistic, Chaldean, Chinese, and Vedic numerology are all different. If you work with number power, you're best off choosing a single system and sticking to it.

Planets, signs, and planetary hours are another example of things that can be considered to have inherent natural or supernatural power, and many people do their magic carefully, calculating the planetary hour before proceeding. Color magic is another area where it's not exactly clear if the power is natural or supernatural—and it doesn't really matter!

Any of these "supernatural things" work on a sympathetic level, creating symbolic sympathy with the intended subject. In addition, though, they have, or may have, inherent occult power just as other supernatural and natural power sources do.

Saved, Accumulated, or Stored Power

How do you store up power for later use? This is one of the most common ways of accessing power, one with lots of folklore and even pop culture backing its use.

Power can simply be absorbed, and thus accumulated, by happenstance. Things that are hanging around where magic is done might start feeling tingly, acquiring a bit of a charge. In my experience, minerals—stones, metals, salts, and bone—tend to hold on to power more readily than something like cloth or leather. But even a ceremonial robe, perhaps originally worn for convenience, can, over time, start to feel magical, like there's a little bit of juice stored it in.

A robe that is purposely used for magic is almost a **magical tool**. So let's discuss tools next. I've been mentioning them all along—it's kind of hard to talk even briefly about magic without noting that a wand or an athame might be part of the process. Magical tools gain power in a few ways.

First, a tool is *created* in order to be magical. As you create it, you are imbuing the tool with mental energy—power from the mind, heart, and spirit. You are concentrating on its creation, thinking about magic and about using the tool. You are transcending time: in the present, you are creating the tool, but simultaneously your mind is working with the tool in the future. Obviously, this is a recommendation to make your own tools. Certainly specialized tools—knives and swords come to mind—require a specialized skill set, but you can still customize your tool in some way, feeding your energy into the process of creation. Some people make or finish all of their tools in ritual space to increase the effect of this concentration and focus.

A tool might be a found object, which can also be personalized by you. There is also the deliberate mental process of choosing that found object *as* a tool; your energy is in the choice you've made.

Next, a tool is usually charged or consecrated, sometimes to a specific purpose. Here, you are again using your focused mind and will, as well as spoken words (which we'll get to in a bit), to bring about a transformed and energized state.

I have a sistrum I made and consecrated to the specific purpose of evoking the Goddess at the full moon. That's all that instrument does, and all it has done for many years. I think, just reading that, you might feel the power of the instrument. Setting something aside and reserving it for a special use allows the power to accumulate more effectively.

Here's the thing: objects in general absorb the energy of their surroundings. This is why some psychics can hold an object and tell you something about its owner. (This is known as *psychometry*.) It's why some old object from your former home might *feel like* that home. The feeling is partially a result of your own memories and associations, of course, but there can be more to it than that.

So when you segregate something so that it is only used for one kind of thing, the energy it acquires naturally, simply by existing, is only from that one thing, and that applies to evoking the Goddess every bit as much as it does to wearing your lucky golf shoes.

When you consecrate an object, it can declare that segregation and begin the process of separating out that particular sort of energy. That's not all a consecration does, of course. In general, it's a cleansing, removing energy that is unwanted or unconnected to the tool's purpose. It also brings energy into the object.

A consecration is almost always performed by using other energies—natural and supernatural ones, perhaps power from deities, if you call upon them, as well as power from the self. It's typical to consecrate a tool using the four (or five) elements. As described in the "Elemental Power" section earlier, the usual procedure is to wet the tool with saltwater while declaring your intention to consecrate by earth and water, then pass the tool through incense smoke, again declaring intent, to consecrate by fire and air.

It's also typical to consecrate a tool with an already consecrated one—touching a new wand to a consecrated wand, for example. Magical contagion is obviously in effect here, but so is stored power.

Here's an easy question: Which is more powerful, a brand-new wand or one you've had for years? Both hold the power of consecration, but only one has been in use, in a magical space, accumulating energy year after year, spell after spell, ritual after ritual.

Being in use empowers a tool, and you can add to that deliberately. When I finish a ritual, I sometimes find that I feel charged up, full of excess energy, perhaps ungrounded. At such times, I pick up my athame and send the excess energy into it while grounding myself. It's like packing up leftovers and putting them in the freezer—it's there for later use.

So magical tools gain power four ways: from being created, from being consecrated, from being used, and perhaps from having additional power deliberately added to them. There's a fifth source of power, though, which most magical tools contain: historical, archetypal, or cultural power.

I feed energy into my wand when I carve it, when I create it, and when I use it. But Western culture as a whole is continually feeding energy into the thoughtform, or archetype, of "magic wand."

Anything that has the weight of cultural history behind it carries energy. That is certainly, by the way, a reason *not* to use some things, if that weight is a burden. Think about marriage. There are lots of reasons, both practical and romantic, to marry your life partner. There's also a huge amount of cultural and historical energy flowing into the archetype of "marriage." It's exactly for that reason that marriage is so compelling and desired, and *also* can be so completely unappealing. You don't just get married, you become part of an energy flow, and many people question if they can live within that energy or reshape it to their own ends.

When you do magic, you can use tools, objects, names, or even ideas that have been around for generations or centuries. You can ride the wave of the power that adds to your work.

Exercise 17: Cultural Power

Think for a moment about each of the following words and phrases. What associations does the word have for you? Does the word feel powerful? Does it feel attractive?

- Witch
- Sorcerer
- Wizard
- Wand
- Cauldron
- Magic spell

- Sword
- Chalice
- Tarot
- Astrology
- Crystal ball
- Full moon

These thoughtforms start with power, accumulated through history and culture. A brand-new, never consecrated or used cauldron carries within it the cultural weight of "cauldron." It's the Witches' brew, it's the unending source of nourishment, it's Brigid's flame, it's every cauldron in every fairy tale.

This power is one of the reasons I love tradition, although I know it's not everyone's cup of tea.

One additional source of accumulated power is that which is accumulated from magic itself. A minute ago, I described how I drain power into my athame when I feel supercharged after a ritual. This feeling of excess charge comes about because magic isn't a perfectly efficient system. If it was, you'd raise exactly as much power as you need and use 100 percent of it. But that's not how it works.

Magical energy is left over, not just in the practitioner but in stuff. The leftovers of spells and rituals can become energy-imbued ritual objects themselves.

For example, what do you do with the salt you've used for consecrations in ritual? It can be disposed of and it can be reused in the next ritual, but it can also be added to a ritual bath or to ritually prepared food, or sprinkled on your doorstep for protection.

Another example is one often taken advantage of by Tantric magicians, and that is sexual fluids. If you've done sex magic, the bodily fluids that are a part of sex are imbued with the power of the ritual and are used to consecrate talismans and the like. You might find this particular example icky and choose not to adopt the practice, but the power is undeniable.

A Magical Tool Set

There are a myriad of things people use as magical tools. The basic set of "necessary" tools varies according to the magical tradition you practice or are influenced by.

Are tools necessary? Many people like to say something like, "The only tool you really need is your mind." That's sort of true, but as we've seen, tools are a source of power for several reasons. The only transportation device you really need is your feet, but a bicycle or car will get you there faster and you won't be as worn-out when you arrive.

Because I *do* love tradition, and because tradition brings a unique power, I think it's worth presenting traditional tools here. I have been referring to them throughout this text, and will continue to do so, even though their use is entirely optional.

There are four tools that are most common in Western magic. You'll find them in most traditions of Wicca, in other forms of Witchcraft, in the Golden Dawn, and in most ceremonial magic. They are the four suits of the tarot, and in most tarot decks you'll see them as the tools used by the Magician.

Sword/Dagger/Athame: In the tarot, the suit is "swords," but as a rule of thumb, a personal knife is considered the equivalent of a sword for most magical uses. The sword is considered to correspond to air or fire, depending on your magical system. It's considered male and phallic. In some Hermetic schools of thought, the sword is considered "active male," meaning it is male in shape (phallic) and in materials (steel/iron) and so represents unadulterated or untampered male energy. It can also be seen as representing heterosexual male energy, or "butch" male energy.

The dagger or athame is a personal blade, while the sword is more typically used for a group working. Traditionally, both are double-edged and straight, and the hilt of a Wiccan's athame is usually black.

The dagger or sword is used mainly for three things. First, it is used to direct energy. Any time you might point your hands to send energy, you could hold your dagger and point it instead. My teacher really hated when people had curved blades for this reason—she felt that since the shortest distance between two points is a straight line, an athame's blade should direct the energy to flow in a straight line.

Second, a blade is used to summon and command, as when you summon an elemental or spirit. Third, a blade is used to demarcate space. The sharp edge cuts ritual space apart from mundane space.

Wand: The wand corresponds to fire or air—whichever *isn't* the sword in the tradition being worked. It's considered male and phallic. In Hermetics, the wand is "passive male" and as such is traditionally made from a female wood such as willow (tree lore is a whole separate topic). It is male energy infused with female energy and can also correspond to gay male energy, or two-spirit energy with a male presentation, or "femme" or "swish" male energy.

Wands, like athames, direct energy. They are used whenever a blade might be considered too aggressive, and for many magicians, the wand is the primary tool.

Cup: The cup corresponds to water and is considered yonic and female. As the "active female" tool, it should be made from a female material (silver or pewter) or, if ceramic, glazed or painted a female color. It is the opposite complement to the dagger and can be considered to correspond to heterosexual female energy, or "femme" female energy.

The cup is used to receive and direct water energy, to drink (especially to partake of consecrated drinks), and to make offerings.

Pentacle: The pentacle is a flat disk with symbols marked or engraved on it. It corresponds to the element of earth. As the "passive female" tool, it should be made from a male material (gold or bronze) or be a male color. It is female energy infused with male energy. It can be considered the bearer of gay female energy, or two-spirit energy with a female presentation, or "butch" female energy.

The pentacle is used as a plate, for partaking of or offering consecrated foods, and to transmit earth energy.

Other tools used by magical practitioners include:

- Stang
- Ankh
- Scourge
- Bell
- Staff
- Sickle
- Boline or white-handled knife
- Broom or besom
- Cingulum or cord
- Aspergillum
- Crystal
- Cauldron
- Hammer
- Censer

Accessing Saved/Accumulated/Stored Power

One of the reasons that stored power is popular is because it's so easy to access—just use the tool or other item! This may be why folklore and pop culture love the concept so much. If you find the right magic object, all you have to do is pick it up. Rub the lamp, open the book, drink the potion … fiction is full of examples of magic just sitting there in an object, waiting to be used.

I'm a big fan of simplicity, and in this case it's justified. From chapter 1 we know that power is only one of the things that makes magic work, and we've spent plenty of time going over what else is needed. But to access *this* power, just pick up the already powerful tool and use it in your ritual. You don't even have to concentrate or focus, meaning that this extra power is accessible to you while you're focused intently on other things.

Power can also be purposely placed into an object, for later release. We'll cover this when we discuss sending power in chapter 7.

Magic Words

I decided to put magic words in their own separate category because they don't have a single source of power. Rather, the power can be from any number of sources, depending upon the specific words and how they are used.

Magic words are a means of accessing power from the *mind*, because of the effect of meaning on your brain and because of the effect of artistry, and of beauty. Words also have an impact on memory. Words can draw power from the *body* because of the ways in which words resonate when spoken, vibrating in the chest and throat and drawing upon breath. Words may also have *rhythm*, which acts on both body and mind. Certain words, in many traditions, are believed to come directly from *deity*, or from angels or other *supernatural beings*, and so draw upon those sources of power. And many words draw upon *accumulated* or *stored* power—especially from historical or archetypal sources.

Since power from words comes from pretty much every place we've already discussed, it makes sense to discuss them apart from any particular source.

There's no need to talk about how to access the power of words: You speak them. Simply saying the words unlocks the power inherent in them, although—and this is important—you should *say* them.

Speaking aloud and thinking words to yourself are two entirely different things. There's good, solid neuroscience behind that: Verbalizing fires many more neural synapses, in more parts of the brain, than thinking does. The thought has to travel to the speech center of the brain, and as it travels, brain cells light up.

Have you ever gone to someone for help with a problem, told her the problem, and immediately seen a solution—even before the other person had a chance to say a word? The very act of speaking aloud opened your mind in ways merely thinking could not. In addition, the physical effect of speech, the impact of breath and vibration, doesn't occur when you merely think the words.

So even if you are doing solitary ritual, speak out loud.

Incantations, Rhymes, Charms, and Spells

> *Double, double toil and trouble;*
> *Fire burn and cauldron bubble.*
> *Cool it with a baboon's blood,*
> *Then the charm is firm and good.*[14]

The original meaning of "spell" in magic is the same as that of a charm or incantation—they are all words that describe forms of verbal magic. An "incantation" is chanted or intoned, a "spell" is spelled out (usually written, but it can refer

---

14. William Shakespeare, *Macbeth*, act 4, scene 1.

to spoken words), and a "charm" is a magical object such as a talisman, but also the words used to seal the magic, as Shakespeare gives us here.

Incantations create cadence of speech, and the tempo and rhythm become part of the power. Repetition and rhyme help you remember the words to say, and create a low-level trance that can be part of the power being raised. Think about the Shakespeare quote—you probably knew it before you saw it here, because it rhymes, because it uses repetition (*double, double*), and because of its cultural familiarity.

Rhythm and rhyme allow you to speak the words of a spell without having to think about it much, and repetition allows you to circle round and round with the words, raising more and more power without ever having to stop and ask what you're supposed to say next.

Here's a simple rhyme:

> *By count of one, the spell is done.*
> *By count of two, the spell comes true.*
> *By count of three, so mote it be!*

It rhymes, you'll never forget it, and you can say it over and over as you do other work to raise power, such as dance, drum, or stir a cauldron. You can adapt the words, changing "the spell" for your specific work, and "count" for whatever you're doing. (*By beat of one, new job is won. By beat of two, new job comes true.*) You can add four or five or whatever number of lines if you have more that must be said.

Words such as these help draw power from mind and body, they help focus your intense desire and passion, and they can keep you moving with a rhythm. They also serve to draw a group of people together when working as a group—

they keep you all on the same beat, moving, thinking, feeling, *intending* together.

Calls

A call is a simple word or phrase spoken, often shouted, during power raising. It can be used as a kind of focal point in a spell. For example, in the previous counting spell, I swapped out "the spell" for "new job." A call would be used by shouting "New job!" or just "Job!" while raising power. A call can be shouted on a beat, or it can be random, as you're moved, while power builds. Typical calls include the name of the person receiving the magic or a single word representing the goal.

One of the great things about using calls is they help you condense your thoughts and feelings about the work you're doing into that single word. Ambiguity is the enemy of magic, so getting your mind to focus on this single word, and figuring out what that word should be, is powerful.

Prayers

Prayers are "magic words" that evoke, call upon, and draw the attention of a deity. You can open your working with a prayer, asking a deity to send power. You can incorporate a prayer into a power-raising, using it as your incantation. You can pray instead of doing other power-raisings.

Affirmations

Do affirmations belong in a book about magic? They are decidedly New Agey for an occult book, that's for sure. On the other hand, magic is about effecting change, and affirmations are words used to do exactly that.

In fact, I think of an affirmation as a kind of spell. In chapter 8, we'll define the components of a spell in detail, and we'll see then that affirmations have all of these components. We've already defined the basic steps of performing a spell more than once, though: focus, connect, raise power, send power, finish.

An affirmation is a spell in which the words of the spell are the "raise power" component.

The construction of an affirmation is interesting. And magical. It asserts that something is true. Presumably, the only reason you're using the affirmation is because there's a mundane reality in which it *isn't* true (although you can use affirmations to maintain, rather than create, a truth).

For example, I might repeat fifteen times each day, out loud, while looking into a mirror:

> *People notice my skills and reward them.*

What is happening here? Let's assert that people haven't been noticing or rewarding my skills, and that's why I'm making this daily effort. But I don't say *I want* people to reward me. I'm using magical language, and magical language works by creating a reality—an assumption of success—as we've discussed. In fact, in a magical understanding of language, if you looked into the mirror and said daily, *I want people to notice my skills and reward them*, that's exactly what you'd create—you'd create *that you want* this to happen. It's very important, anytime you use magical words, that the **words assert the reality you are creating**.

Look at the previous counting rhyme. It is done. It is true. So mote it be. All of this language asserts that the spell *has already worked*. This hearkens back to what we have learned about transcending time. The spell works now, today, in this timeless eternal moment. We are not working toward a future, we are manifesting a present.

So an affirmation uses magical language to transcend time. It uses repetition to raise power and perhaps alter consciousness. It can (optionally) use magical numbers in the repetitions.

Barbarous Words

The phrase "barbarous words" or "barbarous names" comes from the Greek, and originally referred to "foreign" words—anything not Greek was a barbarous tongue.

> *Such barbarous words were considered powerful simply because they came from another language—they had an inherent strangeness that made them salient and "weird."*[15]

In magic, the term refers to any magic word, phrase, spell, or name that has an unknown meaning or, perhaps, is meaningless. Many old spells consisting of barbarous words may be bastardized Egyptian, Hebrew, or another language, mistranslated, miscopied, or misheard. Some are based on magical languages such as Enochian. Some barbarous words may have been invented, knowing they were meaningless, in order to have magical effect. The idea—and it is an ancient one—is that it is the sound of the words that is powerful, not the meaning, and so the words should *not* be translated into English (or whatever language the magician speaks) even if the meaning is discerned.

---

15. Patrick Dunn, *Magic, Power, Language, Symbol: A Magician's Exploration of Linguistics* (Woodbury, MN: Llewellyn, 2008), 110.

Many magical practitioners firmly insist that it is a mistake to ever use words that you don't understand. Indeed, that's prudent advice. If you don't know what you're saying, it seems quite possible that you could invoke something or someone you had no intention of calling, or otherwise manifest a reality contrary to your wishes. We're back to "The Sorcerer's Apprentice," biting off more than we can magically chew.

But I confess I've always been fascinated by the idea of a magical language, one that has power without being understood. Perhaps this comes from my childhood in Judaism. I listened to Hebrew prayers in synagogue, but didn't understand them. Obviously, Hebrew isn't a "barbarous tongue"—it's simply another language. But liturgical language has power when it's not understood—not *despite* not being understood, but *because* of it. I've attended Reformed synagogues where the entire service was translated into English. To me, it was somehow drained of some of the religious feeling—some of the magic.

I grew up in northern New Jersey, a heavily Catholic area. In the 1980s, there was one Catholic church in the area that offered Latin mass. People drove many miles to attend, passing a dozen or more Catholic churches to attend that one. The language was magical—and I feel confident that the vast majority of people making the trip spoke no Latin.

The power of language when it transcends meaning is extraordinary. It allows us to use our minds in a way that bypasses cognition entirely. It connects us to something deeper and more mysterious. It is, perhaps, this mystery that barbarous words draw upon.

Flavors of Power

Is all power just "power"? Whatever power is—and we gave up on the science of it chapters ago—it seems to start in a pretty undifferentiated manner. Especially when it is raised from our own bodies, the buzz, the *oomph*, feels pretty much the same whether raised slowly or rapidly, alone or in a group.

I have talked for years about "flavors" of power—I suspect I got the phrase from Isaac Bonewits. Flavor is a good metaphor for the different sorts of power. Another might be *tune* or *melody*, as in fine-tuning the power, or having it be "on key." My favorite, lately, is to think of power as a stem cell.

> *Although stem cells do not serve any one function,*
> *many have the capacity to serve any function*
> *after they are instructed to specialize.*[16]

To me, this fascinating description of stem cells is exactly analogous to magical power. Power may come forth in an amorphous manner, being "just power," but it can specialize once instructed.

How to Give Power a Flavor

How does power get a flavor? You can simply "instruct" it, using your willpower and perhaps your words to tell the power what it is.

Here are a bunch of examples of instructing or flavoring power. You can incorporate the motif into a spell or rhyme. For example, if you chanted, spoke, or wrote "Gentle breeze, blow away trouble" as part of a spell, you'd be instructing the

_____

16. Peter Crosta, "What Are Stem Cells?," Medical News Today, last updated on July 19, 2013, www.medicalnewstoday.com/info/stem_cell.

energy to be gentle, and you'd be imbuing it with the qualities of a breeze. If you are working with elements, this adds air energy to your power-raising.

Words in general are a great way to tune your power. When I raise power with music, I am careful to choose a chant or song with lyrics consistent with the power I want to raise.

There is a famous Goddess chant by Deena Metzger that begins "Isis, Astarte…" and continues through cross-cultural goddess names. Raising power with this chant tunes the power toward Goddess worship in general, and toward the energies of those goddesses in particular.

Prayer tunes the energy by request. Prayer flavors the energy with a worshipful quality and also allows the deity or deities to tune the energy as they will.

The source of power often flavors the power, so power from nature will impart a natural quality to the power, and the appropriate element(s) will be present. Power raised in the mountains is earthier, while power raised at the ocean is more watery. Finding an incantation in a book could give power a kind of intellectual or academic flavor.

Why Give Power a Flavor?

Once I was discussing a particular spell with some other experienced Witches. This healing, I explained, should be water energy, gently flowing over the illness (which I then went on to pinpoint). Avoid fire energy, I said, because fire tends to inflame the nerves, and the patient was suffering from severe neuropathy. One Witch asked, "Can't we just send, y'know, *healing* energy?"

Honestly, I was kind of appalled. That's like asking a doctor if you can't just have, y'know, *medicine*, rather than a specific prescription.

As with a stem cell, you instruct your power to specialize because your magic is specific. In chapter 8, we'll get into details about why and how spells must be specific. But let's look at two aspects of it here, things that relate directly to the idea of flavoring or instructing power.

First, , flavoring power affects the mind of the magician. You have worked on your mind skills from chapter 4 in order to have fixed intention on your purpose. You don't want your method of raising power to cause cognitive dissonance.

Sex magic raises sex-flavored energy. If you're seeking a job in the banking industry, sex-flavored energy is radically inconsistent with your intention, and so, when you're focusing your intention, it will be dissonant. On the other hand, textile magic has ancient associations with domesticity and would bring the right flavor to magic on behalf of a new home.

So flavor helps intention. Flavor also helps in sending energy toward the target; it aligns with purpose. As you send energy (which we will cover in the next chapter), you'll find that the energy will have an affinity for a target with similar energy—like attracts like. So chaotic, fiery energy is naturally drawn toward a chaotic, fiery target.

Finally, don't forget that energy is *real*. In the example I started with, of a healing spell needing to be gentle, I was talking about the real-world repercussions that energy has on its target. Have you ever seen that cartoon by S. Harris with a formula on a blackboard, the statement "Then a miracle occurs," then more formula? The punch line is "I think you should be more explicit here in step two." People sometimes look at magic like that—step one, do the spell; step two, THEN A MIRACLE OCCURS; step three, result.

The fact is, there's a step two. The energy arrives. It does something. When you're doing a healing, it is generally true that the patient feels the energy—he may not know what it is, but he feels it. So your energy should be flavored not only in accordance with exactly what the patient needs, but also to accommodate exactly what he can tolerate. *Especially* when someone has nerve pain, sending hot, forceful, rah-rah energy is too much for that person to take.

Power Flavors by Source

This is by no means a definitive list—more like an inspiration, or discussion material. But here are the powers discussed in this chapter and the previous one, and the kind of flavors that might be imparted by raising power in this way:

- **Power Raised from Deity:** This kind of power is flavored by worshipfulness, perhaps by humility, and is used for theurgy, for acts of mercy, or for help with personal goals in which the deity may be invested. When power is raised by evoking specific Pagan deities, that power can have almost any energy, since such deities themselves specialize. Examples include Brigid for creativity-flavored work, Sarasvati for education-flavored work, or Thor for weather working.

- **Power Raised from Emotion:** This type of power is flavored by the emotion: passionate energy for passionate purposes, loving energy for love magic, and so on.

- **Power Raised from Meditation or Concentration:** There is no inherent flavor to this type of power, which can be used for anything with the exception of purposes around letting go, around not thinking, and around wildness. Concentration on spontaneity is not a natural fit.

- **Power Raised from Movement:** This kind of power is imitative of movement in general, and can help with anything that is "stuck," be it emotions or career. Movement can express and create a flavor of joy and freedom; those flavors can work toward personal-fulfillment targets that need those feelings. Movement can instruct the energy to give a vitality to the physical body and thus heal through imitative magic.

- **Sex Magic:** Flavored by sex, pleasure, and sometimes fertility, sex magic is effective in any attraction spell. Certainly it can attract lovers, but it can be effective even for something less sexy, like companionable neighbors or a bass player for your band, because "attraction" isn't always sensual in nature. A couple can do sex magic toward things they want to do together as a couple, like being able to take a vacation.

- **Pain Magic:** Flavored by intensity and sacrifice, this type of power can be used in any emergency situation, for help in a crisis, when the emergent nature of the goal matches the level of pain. The flavor can also be worshipful, giving oneself over to the deity, and so is good for theurgy. **Austerities** have a similar flavor.

- **Aura Work and Rhythm:** Both of these kinds of power are fairly "neutral" in terms of flavor and can be used for almost any spell. Rhythm is excellent for cardiac-related healing work. Aura work, flavored by touch without touch actually occurring, is excellent for distant healing and love work.

- **Textile Magic:** As previously mentioned, textile magic has a domestic quality that is excellent for things related to the home, marriage, or fertility. Bringing things together (as if sewn together) is also energetically and sympathetically connected to textile work.

- **Nature as a Whole, and Natural Things:** The flavor of this kind of power is consistent with the feeling of or the metaphorical relationship to the natural feature. Ocean magic is rhythmic like the tides; it is connected to the element of water, it is mysterious and "deep," and it is connected to the source of life (life evolved in the sea). Likewise, mountain magic is connected to the elements of earth (the mountain) and air (the altitude). It is connected to isolation and wisdom (metaphorically—like going up to the mountains on retreat, or the Hermit card in the tarot, alone on a mountaintop).

- **Elements:** Elements are sources of power and are flavors—Water (or watery) is the flavor of water magic. You'll find a list of qualities and correspondences for each element in appendix A.

- **Accumulated or Stored Power:** This type of power is flavored by the object in which the power is stored. You'll find a list of tool correspondences in appendix A.

Exercise 18: Flavors of Magic

1. Make a list of the kinds of spells you think you might do, things you want that you think you might achieve via magic.

2. For each spell on the list, describe its flavor.

3. For each spell/flavor, name a type of power-raising that would help impart that flavor.

seven

Sending Power

The subject of how to send power may seem obvious at first. Two full chapters on raising power have value that seems apparent—there are many sources of power and many ways of raising it. But sending power? Most people think of it as sort of automatic: You raise the power until it hits a point of intensity, where it feels you're at the maximum or it feels like "this is it," and then you send it. Whoosh. You might think that's all there is to it, making a chapter on the subject superfluous.

In fact, there are a number of different ways to send power, and advantages and disadvantages to each. Naturally, there are also plenty of tips and tricks one learns along the way that improve power-sending technique. Some of this discussion will combine power raising with power sending, so that, while we previously learned about the kinds of power that can be raised and where power comes from, now we'll talk about the process from beginning to end. Some of this chapter might be called "raise and send," but that sounds kind of awkward, so let's stick with what we have.

We'll start by talking about *where* and *whether* to send power, and then we'll go over various methods of *how*.

Target and Goal

Target and goal are the most important concepts to understand in order to determine where you are sending power and where you are focusing your intention and concentration.

When you send energy, it is generally because you have a goal. Here is a list of fairly typical goals for which people frequently do magic:

- Finding love
- Healing (physical, emotional, spiritual)
- Protection
- Finding a job
- Real estate goals (finding a home, selling a home, keeping a home)
- Improving relationships (in romance, in a family, at work, in friendship)
- Connecting to people (finding members for your coven/band/club, finding friends)

- Self-actualization
- Spiritual goals (worship, invocation, evocation)
- Weather magic (especially delaying rain for special events)

There are plenty of other reasons to do magic, but I think this covers 90 percent of what people do. Everything on this list is a goal or a category of goals. These are *why* you do magic. They are not *where* you send power.

Imagine that you practice archery and you are trying to win a medal. The goal is the medal. The target is the round thing with the bull's-eye on it. It's very important that you shoot your arrow at the target and not at the goal—if you shoot the arrow at the goal, you might hit a judge, and that would be bad.

People who practice magic can sometimes be bad archers. They have a goal in mind, but not a target. I'll tell you right now that there are occult teachers who advise against having a specific target. They'll tell you that the gods should choose *how* the magic will work, and our job as human practitioners is merely to send energy into the request.

It is true that sometimes we can't accurately pick a target, that sometimes we have to ask that the energy find a way to an appropriate target despite our shortcomings. Our target may be metaphorical—a path out of a problem, for example. But we have already determined that magic and prayer are different—I'd suggest that sending energy to the gods and just letting them figure out the rest more strongly resembles prayer than magic.

How Do You Pick a Target?

Since I've already offered an entire list of goals, let's start by figuring out what a target might be in a magical working. In fact, choosing the target is a crucial part of determining how to instruct or flavor your energy and what kind of spell you'll be doing.

Basically, **figure out where the magic has to go to be effective**. What is it that has to change? The goal is the desired change, but the target should be the locus of change.

Suppose your buddy Mondo has a tumor. The goal is *healthy, whole Mondo*. What's the target?

- If you target the *tumor*, you are sending shrinking, diminishing, or blasting power directly into the tumor.
- If you target the *surgeon*, you're imbuing her with skill and deftness, with an eagle eye, with the ability to miss nothing and get every cancer cell, while leaving Mondo well able to recover.

You are not targeting "wellness." Wellness is the *goal*. If Mondo is doing a course of chemo first, then targeting the tumor makes sense, but if he's having immediate surgery, then you're probably working on the surgeon. In this example, the decision is relatively easy.

How about love magic? Many people say flat out that love magic is unethical, for the simple reason that the wrong kind of love spell can be manipulative or controlling. Don't ever sleep with someone who is not capable of giving enthusiastic consent! Just as too much alcohol or drugs can render a person incapable of giving consent, too much unethical magic can do the same.

However, an appropriate target of a love spell is *yourself.* In the "real world," if you desired a particular someone, you'd do your best to make yourself more attractive to her. This might include things about you, such as dressing better and wearing perfume, and it might include things about her, such as being in places where you could "happen" to bump into each other, or seeing her favorite movie so that the two of you could discuss it. Love spells that target the free will of the object of your affections lack her consent, just as abducting her would, but spells that target yourself and your own attractiveness, or that target proximity or happy coincidences, are entirely ethical. So while the goal might be the two of you together, the proper, ethical target is yourself, and the power should be flavored with attraction.

Specific Target

The more narrowly you target your magic, the greater the likelihood of success.

A lot of people choose a vague target on purpose. Some, as previously described, think the target should be chosen by the gods or by the universe. Others, though, seem to think a bigger target is easier to hit. That's true: If you're aiming for the side of the barn, you're more likely to "succeed" than if you're aiming for a small door-shaped space on the side of the barn. On the other hand, if the goal is to create a door, aiming for something door-shaped is going to produce a better result.

Your energy is finite. If you splatter it everywhere, there's less to go around. If you paint the whole barn with the amount of paint you have for painting the door, your coverage just won't be as good, your color won't be as rich, and some spots won't get any paint at all. Think of your magical energy like that paint.

We want Mondo's surgeon to target Mondo's tumor very specifically. We don't want her just chopping away at his body and hoping for the best. Magically, we should target Mondo's tumor equally specifically and not just send healing energy in his general direction.

Choosing a specific target is the best way to make sure the energy goes exactly where you want it to go. It's also the best way to truly take responsibility for your own magic. After all, if you raise a lot of power and then vaguely send it "out there," it's not really your fault if nothing happens. No one can claim it didn't get where it was going if "where it was going" was left open-ended. When you fully own your magic and commit to it, as you do when you specify a target in detail, you will be greatly empowered. It's a scary step to take, but an important one.

Finally, choosing a specific target *and* goal helps you figure out what you really want. Often, we wish for something better in life without grasping that wish, looking at it closely, and determining what it really is. When you commit to specificity in magic, you actually discover a great deal about yourself, because you need that information in order to proceed.

Local Target

Part of pinpointing your goal and target is found in being local. By this I mean a local place, local people, and local things.

People have been doing the "visualize world peace" thing for quite a while now, and the world remains resolutely nonpeaceful. However, magic seems to have a noticeable effect on the local level.

The Maharishi University of Management—founded by Maharishi Mahesh Yogi, who is also the founder of Transcendental Meditation (TM)—has reported a "Maharishi Effect," where crime rates are reduced in the city where TM is practiced, as compared to cities where practitioners are less prevalent. The first study on this effect was reported in 1976, but was discredited. However, there have been several studies since, including an intriguing one in 1993 in Washington, DC.

Here's the concept: Don't look at world peace. Look at the effect that a local group raising energy has on that locality. Look at the city, or better yet, look at the neighborhood.

Remember, too, that all of the studies that have been done have been focused on the effects of *meditation*. The idea is that simply generating the mental/spiritual energy creates a local impact. When you do magic, you're not talking about the effect as a byproduct, but as the whole point of the exercise.

If I wanted to reduce violent crime in my immediate neighborhood (a local and specific goal), how would I go about it? Perhaps I could create a cloud of peacefulness that would cover and permeate a radius of several blocks. My target, then, is the cloud, and my energy flavor is peaceful and kind of sticky. The goal and target are complex and ambitious, but notice how being local and specific helps: The magic is understandable and potentially achievable, and my mind can accept it. I know what I'm doing, why, and (more or less) how. "Visualize world peace" has none of those qualities.

This doesn't mean that you can't do distance magic. Naturally, you have to establish a sympathetic connection whenever you perform magic, and you have easy, natural sympathy with your own locality. But because you've learned that magic transcends time and space, you are not confined to your own neighborhood, region, or state. The idea of "local" is about physically narrowing the parameters of the goal.

So if you're working on Mondo's surgeon, you should know what hospital she's in. If you are casting a blessing over peace talks, you should know the city in which those talks are taking place and localize your energies.

Knowledge Is Power

In the previous paragraph, I used the phrase "you should know" twice. Knowledge is crucial to empowering your magic, and knowledge of the goal and target is key to a successful spell.

The more you know, the better you can target. If we return to our archery analogy, it's obvious that a target you can see clearly is easier to hit than one you cannot see at all or can only see vaguely.

One spell I did as a beginner was to help a pregnant friend. I knew she had serious health concerns about the baby, and she'd stopped answering her phone (this was way back before cell phones, email, or social media). I worked intensively to save the pregnancy, but I eventually found out that she'd already miscarried before I did my magic. All other efforts—power raised, sympathy created, space transcended so as to reach her in Florida when I was in New York—were immaterial because I didn't realize the goal was no longer achievable.

Here are some of the things we should know before doing magic:

- What is the goal?
- Can the goal be achieved?
- *Should* the goal be achieved?
- Who or what is the target?
- Where is the target?
- What are the potential repercussions of achieving the goal?
- Is magic needed?

So, for my friend's pregnancy, the goal was to carry to term, and that goal could not be achieved.

What about "should" the goal be achieved? Often, we are looking from the outside at complex situations. We know we want to help, but perhaps we don't know how. Our friends' relationship is troubled. Is it best to work for reconciliation, or are these two people better off apart? A friend is in a custody dispute. Are we confident which home is best for the children? A relative has slipped into a coma. Do we work for healing or for an easy, painless passage to the other side?

Sometimes answers seem unknowable. Perhaps the person in a coma discussed his wishes with you previously, but often that is not the case.

Divination is an important tool for any practitioner of magic. It can help you determine the appropriate goal and target, whether or not magic can or should be done, and help you focus and flavor your energies. When a spell has a significant unknown factor in the mix, pull out your tarot deck, rune stones, or scrying mirror. The method isn't important.

What *is* important is that you draw upon your magical skills to answer questions before proceeding, if those questions have an impact on what you will do or how you will do it.

What do I mean by repercussions? I think all of us have been in situations in which we had to deal with the unintended consequences of well-meaning actions. It's important to understand that you won't be able to anticipate *every* potential result of your magic, and you shouldn't let that stop you from doing the work. Nonetheless, a careful examination of what you're doing *and what happens next* matters.

Weather working is a perfect example. Pushing complex weather systems around willy-nilly isn't necessarily good for the environment. Sure, you want it to be sunny for your outdoor event, but is the rain needed? Perhaps you can focus your magic to move clouds to a specific nearby location, or to delay the rain by only a few hours. Healing can also have unintended consequences. In medicine, a patient's need for treatment must be balanced by that patient's ability to tolerate the treatment; a weak, infection-prone person may not be able to have surgery even if that surgery offers a cure. Similarly, blasting a person in delicate health with a massive wave of healing energy may not be well tolerated. Your magic may need to be tempered; an emergency doesn't necessarily require speed and intensity.

Is magic needed? I raise this subject because of the memorable occasion when an acquaintance requested healing energy be sent to help him get over a head cold. I was, quite honestly, annoyed. There are so many worthy purposes and only so many hours in the day to devote to sending power.

Why do so for an illness that is guaranteed to pass on its own fairly quickly and leave no lasting damage? While that may be a silly example, there are certainly occasions when a little research would help you understand whether magic is actually called for. This is kind of the positive flip side of "is it achievable?" In the case of my friend's miscarriage, the magic should not have been done because of a preexisting negative outcome. What about a preexisting positive outcome? The missing child has already been found, the baby has already been born healthy, the weather report changed and rain is no longer expected. Sometimes, when I'm about to do a spell, I'll make a phone call for an up-to-the-minute update. Is he out of surgery or is surgery happening now? Is there a fever? Has the specific area of concern changed? If ritual preparations run late, your last-minute call could bring the news "out of surgery and out of danger," in which case perhaps magic is no longer needed, or you could focus instead on helping with the recovery process.

Splitting Focus

Focus is required for both raising and sending power. Focus on the goal helps raise power through inspiration, emotional connection, and sympathy. Focus on both goal and target helps flavor the energy. Focus on the target is necessary for sending to that target. There are times, though, when focus is challenging, not because you lack mind skills—having read chapter 4, I assume you've developed yours!—but because there are multiple points of focus, or because the energy being raised has an unfocused quality.

One of the advantages of working with two or more people is that you can split the focus in ways that help address these problems.

Splitting Target and Goal

Let's get back to Mondo. You have to focus on his tumor, pinpointing its exact location in his body, clearly seeing the energy rushing into it, and shrinking it into nothingness.

You *also* have to maintain consciousness of Mondo's wellness—your goal. One way of doing that is to share duties among the participants.

One of the tricky parts of a group working can be to make sure that everyone is visualizing the same way—the energy can't get where it's going if everyone is using a different "where." Here, it helps to know that often a goal doesn't require precision in the way that a target does. "Wellness" can be visualized in a wide variety of ways, but a tumor in a specific location doesn't leave much wiggle room. In a group working, having several people visualize variations on wellness, while one person visualizes the exact target, can be an effective technique. This can be done using the "battery" method, which I will describe shortly. "Variations on wellness" can be such things as focusing on an image of Mondo from before he got sick (perhaps using a photograph), or imagining Mondo doing one of his favorite things, or visualizing him laughing and clearly *hearing* his laugh, or visualizing him doing something he has specifically told you he doesn't currently feel well enough to do, or perhaps picturing him in circle with you, enjoying energy raising with his friends.

Splitting Flavors and Purposes

Sometimes two different flavors of energy are needed—perhaps you wish to visualize a contemplative, sober goal, but the sending of energy should be flavored with ecstatic abandon. In Mondo's case, we want him joyfully healthy, and that joyful tone can infuse the goal. At the same time, the surgeon being targeted should be calm, careful, and precise. If we're targeting the tumor rather than the surgeon, then that shrinking energy is, again, very different from joyful wellness.

Group work allows this division of responsibilities so that simultaneously, two different streams of energy can exist.

The Battery

In *The Way of Four Spellbook*, I described a power-sending method I call the "battery." In terms of how batteries actually work, it's probably a stupid name, but since the previous book is still in print, I'll stick with it.

One person is the "battery"—you might also call him the conductor, the channel, or the conduit. That person has two jobs: to visualize the target and to send the energy to the target.

Everyone else (whether that's a group or just one other person) visualizes the goal and raises and sends power. Power raising and sending can be done using virtually any method.

Power is sent into the battery. *Only the battery sends to the target.*

In general, the battery is the person who is closest to the target or is best able to visualize the target for some other reason. I've had a nurse as the battery for visualizing anatomy (for example, when targeting a cardiac condition), and I've seen a pregnant woman be the battery for a fertility working.

Let's go back to Mondo as an example. There are six of you, and you've chosen to dance to raise power—in part, because dancing is Mondo's favorite thing, and this both creates sympathy and connects energetically to images of Mondo being well.

Five people dance while imagining Mondo well, happy, and dancing.

One person—Mondo's best friend—sits in the center. This person, the battery, visualizes the target (let's say it's the surgeon). This person, too, is raising energy, but is doing so not by dancing but through mental or emotional concentration. He is fixedly seeing the target, and not allowing this vision to waver.

At the appropriate moment, the five dancers send all of their power not to the target but to the battery. The battery takes all their energy, and his own, and sends it to the target.

A number of things have happened here. First, exactly one person has visualized the target and sent the energy to it. That's helpful, because multiple variations on a visualization can sometimes create distortion. Imagine several similar pictures overlaid, one on top of the other; they don't quite sync up. It's like a double-exposure effect; the picture isn't quite clear.

A precisely in-sync visualization isn't always necessary. In the case of Mondo's wellness, visualizations were general and all over the place. That's fine, because "wellness" itself isn't a precise term. In a group, we should all agree in advance as to what we're visualizing and which parts must be precise. Precision is then achieved by exactly one person owning the visualization and the final sending.

Another thing that has happened is that the focus has been split in both of the ways previously described: the group was responsible for the goal, while the battery was responsible for the target, and each gave different flavors to the energy they created. Mondo's wellness and joy carried the surgical excellence to its destination. The battery working allowed two different focuses, and it allowed two different flavors of energy.

In a "burst" sending (which I will describe shortly), the battery is also the person who decides when the power will be sent, or who "calls the drop."

Splitting Power and Focus

Another way to divide the magical duties is between raising the power and doing any visualization at all. When magic is raised through an extreme experience, maintaining focus can be difficult. There are a number of ways to overcome this drawback, but one way is through shared duties.

Sex magic is a great example. When you're caught up in the ecstasy of sensation, picturing your magical target might not be the easiest thing, and picturing that target may not be what you need in order to achieve orgasm.

So how about this: Partner A maintains a clear visualization of the target while bringing Partner B to orgasm. B's entire job is to raise as much sex energy as possible and, at the moment of orgasm, send it all to A. A's job is pretty much the battery job, with the added responsibility of getting B off.

Naturally, B should be an awesome partner and make sure to reciprocate sexually after the sending of power (if A is willing). You can even use this as an opportunity for a second sending of power.

Sex, pain, and certain forms of trance readily lend themselves to this kind of splitting of duties.

Splitting Focus and Power When Working Alone

When you're working alone, how can you split focus? Previously, we split between multiple flavors of energy, we split between focusing on target and focusing on goal, and we split between raising energy and focusing/sending. In each case, we achieved this split by dividing duties among different people. Alone, you have to be a little more creative, and you also have to be a little more methodical.

For splitting flavors of energy, I would raise energy twice, and choose the highest-priority goal first—for example, a wave of slow, methodical energy to Mondo's surgeon, followed by a wave of joy. Raise twice, send twice.

For splitting between raising energy and sending energy, see "Sending Power into Storage" later in this chapter.

My usual technique for splitting the focus between target and goal is to divide between the inner visualization and a focal object.

I can use a picture of Mondo, stare at it, hold it, and so on, while seeing his surgeon in my mind's eye. Or I can do the reverse. Both target and goal are present—one in my visualization and one as an external object. When we talk about sending power into storage, we'll see that the focal object can also be holding power that was sent into it.

When I raise power as a solitary, I usually do so in a way that allows me to maintain this dual focus. For example, drumming or other rhythm allows me to stare at a picture and visualize in my mind.

Words of a chant or call can also be used in splitting focus alone. If I repeat a chant about wellness, I'm using music, repetition, and words of power, and while I'm raising power in this way, I'm also aiding my focus—the words about wellness help keep my mind on a goal of wellness without even concentrating, while I consciously focus on the target.

Sending in a Burst: "Male" Power Sending

When I talk about "male" power sending, I am not talking about anything particularly gendered. It's a method used as often by women and non-binary people as by men. I picked up the terminology from Isaac Bonewits,[17] who likened two kinds of raise-and-release to the way energy moves in male versus female orgasms. Isaac used to speculate that perhaps it's because we live in a patriarchal society that male power sending is the norm in modern magic, especially Wiccan and Neopagan magic.

Male sending follows this pattern: power raising begins gradually, building slowly or quickly but steadily toward a peak, and on the peak, the power is sent all at once, in an intense burst (figure 3). Often, the whole process takes only a few minutes.

A typical Wiccan version of this kind of power sending is used in "raising the cone of power." Witches dance, walk, skip, or run, first slowly, but with increasing tempo, around the circle, chanting, calling, or clapping. Someone "calls the drop," basically shouting "Now!" Everyone drops immediately to the

---

17. Isaac Bonewits, *Rites of Worship: A Neopagan Approach* (Earth Religions Press, 2003), 207.

floor, throwing all the power into the cone, up and out, toward the target.

This kind of power raise-and-send is, at its heart, quite simple. There are a few things, though, that can make it go better. First, allow yourself or yourselves to feel around for a groove before things really get started. To continue the sexual analogy, don't shy away from foreplay! In a group, it can take a few moments before you're all on the same page, using the same beat, feeling the same energy, singing in tune. Even if you're doing something quiet or stationary, finding that sense of unity can come with a few false starts, and that's okay.

For a solitary, the barrier is often self-consciousness. A group may struggle to sync up, but they also give one another confidence. When you're alone, if you falter, there's dead air. If six people drum together and one loses the beat, the other five keep going. It can be harder, alone, when you can't hear that beat maintaining, waiting for you to rejoin, but must "catch up" only with the rhythm in your heart (or perhaps a recording).

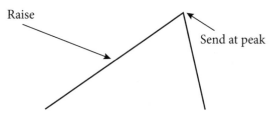

Figure 3: An Ideal Power Raise-and-Send ("Male" Sending)

Figure 4: Peaks and Valleys of Actual Power Raising

Instead of aiming for your power to rise smoothly in a steady line to a peak, allow for some variation, some ups and downs (figure 4).

When I first started practicing magic, those dropping-off points scared me. I would lose confidence that the power would eventually come back up, and I'd send power at a low point, fearing that was as much as we could get. It was a great lesson for me to learn to let go, to trust, to let the power dwindle down to nearly nothing, if need be, and watch as it climbed to a peak more beautiful, more thrilling, than the one that had dropped off and caused me to panic.

Here's another important aspect of this technique: You want to send just *before* the peak, not *at* the peak (figure 5). Look at those final drop-offs. When you're done, the power drops off very fast, pretty much crashing. (Again, the "male" analogy really works.) When you feel the moment coming, when it feels as if the peak will come any second, *send.*

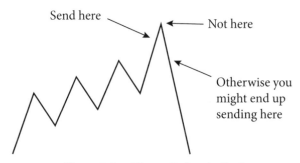

Send here

Not here

Otherwise you
might end up
sending here

Figure 5: Send Power Before the Peak

What if you miscalculate, and the peak comes and the drop-off comes and you didn't send? Should you send during the drop-off? No! Allow that drop-off to become another valley in the jagged climb to the top, catch your breath, let the power climb even higher, and then send. You'll probably be extra-exhausted when you're done, but you'll have sent a powerful stream of energy to your target.

Sending in Waves: "Female" Power Sending

Again, this analogy about gender has nothing to do with the gender of the participants. Female power sending is a technique that replicates how many women have orgasms.

Figure 6: "Female" Power Sent in Waves

Here, the power is raised more gently and more steadily. There is no focus on peaking. Instead, the power rises and falls in waves, and is sent continuously as waves rise (figure 6). There is no need to coordinate sending. There is no "Now!" In a group, people send power as they feel it, and raise and send simultaneously.

During this kind of power raising-and-sending, you will not be going for any kind of build. Power will build naturally; it will flow into high spots, and those spots will become higher and higher, although sometimes, just as in the burst technique, there will be valleys. A wave method of raising and sending may ultimately end in a burst (just as a female orgasm does), but it may also taper off, with waves gradually decreasing just as they gradually increased.

Wave sending can be maintained for a long period of time. In order to effectuate timelessness, I never use a watch or clock during a magical ritual, but I'd guess that I've maintained this kind of power sending for thirty or forty-five minutes. It's quite effective in combination with a trancey or meditative power-raising, or with a raising that is of necessity slow, such as certain kinds of textile magic.

Sending Power into Storage

Power can be sent somewhere and stored there. This power can be raised and sent in a burst or wave, as just described. When it is sent into an object, this object then becomes a source of stored power, as described in the previous chapter.

Talismans

A talisman is a magical object made to be worn or carried for a particular purpose. There are many names for such magical objects—charms, amulets, jujus, fetishes, etc.—and each is slightly different. A talisman is something made for a singular magical purpose, often marked with potent symbols and imbued with magical energy.

For example, planetary talismans have various symbols associated with the individual planet, are created during appropriate planetary hours and from appropriate planetary materials, and provide power associated with that planet. So the talisman of Venus protects against jealousy and preserves marital harmony; it has on it a dove (among other things) and is made of copper.

When power is sent into a talisman, the purpose of the magic is fulfilled by wearing, carrying, or otherwise situating the talisman (placing it in the home, burying it, etc.).

Power flow, as we've been considering it up to this point, is more or less this: get the power, raise it, send it toward a target, goal achieved! So, get the power from the self, from an object, or from deity, and send it in a burst or a wave. The target may be distant or not.

Here, though, the target is an intermediary. Suppose your marriage is troubled. You might have a goal of harmony, and send harmony-flavored energy toward you and your spouse. The target is the two of you, or perhaps "my marriage" as a thoughtform, or perhaps your home—filling the home with harmony. With talismanic magic, though, you send the power into the talisman and then wear it, carry it, or place it in your home, where the power does its work.

Some occultists teach that certain talismanic symbols "trap" the power, keeping it cycling within the talisman once placed there. Since there is no such thing as a perpetual motion machine, and entropy is a real thing, you can expect that over time the power will dissipate, no matter how power-ful the symbols are. Power is released (sent), but only very gradually. It's like a room freshener, releasing a tiny bit of its power round the clock but eventually evaporating—simply having it there alters the atmosphere of the room.

You will, in time, wish to renew the power or discard the talisman if it has served its purpose. Keep in mind, though, that your talisman will continue to gain power from your mind as you wear or carry it. Every time you notice the talisman, you'll be reminded of the power-raising, and your memory will give a little extra juice to it. This will not keep the power going indefinitely by itself, but it tends to maintain the power for longer than you'd think.

Burial

One of the uses of burial is as another form of storage. You send power into an object that is buried. (There are other uses of burial in magic as well.)

As with a talisman, the power of something buried dis-sipates gradually—and by the way, a talisman can be the "something" that is buried, but the possibilities are endless. What's unique about burial is its use to send power specifi-cally through a piece of land. The power can be sent continu-ally, by the object being in the ground, or it can be released as the object rots or disintegrates or otherwise interacts with the earth.

Burying an object filled with protective power is a typi-cal method of protecting a home or other location. It is the magical equivalent of an invisible fence—typical locations for burial are at a property's borders or under the front step.

Knots

Sending power into a knot for storage (again, via a burst or a wave) ties the power up. Imbuing your intention into the power—flavoring it with your purpose—places that purpose into the knot for later release.

While a talisman releases the power gradually, a knot does so all at once. Often, a knot is used as a "just in case" spell. A classic example of this is the folklore custom of Witches knotting up a wind. This practice is noted in Shakespeare's *Macbeth* and is well documented in other sources.[18] The Witch sends power—in this case, wind—into a rope with three knots in it. Untying the first knot releases a gentle breeze. Untying the second knot releases a strong, stiff wind. The third knot releases a hurricane. The ropes were sold to sailors to untie when a wind was needed.

The principle is applicable for plenty of other things besides wind. Certainly, it could be used for other kinds of weather magic. I've never tried tying up "fair weather" in knots, but it seems plausible. A wind has the quality of a *thing*; it seems more concrete than "a nice day," which is sort of nebulous, so I imagine a wind is easier to capture in a knot. I should also warn you that weather magic can be very tricky indeed. When you release a wind or push away rain, that has an effect on the atmosphere: the wind and rain go somewhere, having an impact on surrounding weather systems. It's not easy to control and can have an unfortunate domino effect.

---

18. Olaus Magnus, *A Description of the Northern Peoples* (Rome, 1555).

The Cone of Power

One of the most interesting examples of how power can be sent into storage and then released is the traditional Witch's cone of power. As described earlier in this chapter, the cone of power is raised and sent in a burst. But let's delve more deeply into how it is used.

One of the ideas behind a Wiccan circle is that, once cast, it contains all energy raised within it. The circle holds the energy in, like a pressure cooker, so it can build. Then, when the energy is ready to be released, a "cone of power" is created, all the previously raised energy from the ritual is sent into it, and away it goes. The sending, then, is not just of the power raised during the act of raising the cone, but of all the power raised in the entire ritual.

If a worship circle is held and no thaumaturgy is performed, then releasing the cone of power sends the energy off to the gods for their pleasure. However, if power is raised for a magical purpose, it can be stored in the circle until released by the cone.

This is not a technique I have seen many Wiccans use. Earlier Wiccan literature suggests this use but doesn't describe it as explicitly as I've done here. Most people nowadays seem to go for a power-raising that is immediately sent off, out of the circle, without using the cone. Younger Wiccans may not even be familiar with using a cone at all.

However, in the traditional use of a cone, magic is a two-step process. First, a spell is prepared, as we'll detail in chapter 8. Everything up to the point of raising and sending power is readied in the circle, and perhaps some preliminary power is raised. (This may be referred to as "charging" or "setting" the cone.) Then, at the designated time, the cone of power is raised and the power is sent—for the spell and otherwise. Theoretically, more than one spell could be prepared, and the cone would be raised and sent only once.

The "designated time" is often determined by tradition—that is, a Wiccan tradition will have a set order of liturgy, which may include when the cone of power is created and sent.

The entire concept of two-step spellwork, where raising and sending are separated, is interesting to me. The talisman work of Austin Spare is another example of splitting the creation and execution of a spell into two parts, although Spare's work is significantly more complex.

Austin Osman Spare, a British occultist who briefly studied under Aleister Crowley, developed a method of creating talismans artistically, using letters of the alphabet. Donald Michael Kraig called them "compressed alphabet talismans."[19] As Kraig—the occultist and author who was among the first to combine high magick and Neopaganism in a single work—described it, the talisman is created based on a meaningful word or phrase. Obviously, during the creation of the talisman, the meaning is very much in your mind, and you are pouring mental energy and intention into it. But it is then set aside, and consecrated later. It can actually be consecrated or charged when the original purpose is forgotten! The idea is to allow the subconscious to take over the connection to the spiritual planes.

---

19. Donald Michael Kraig, *Modern Sex Magick: Secrets of Erotic Spirituality* (St. Paul, MN: Llewellyn, 2003), 113–116.

Power sent into storage can be another way of splitting power from focus. Power is raised with concentration and focus and sent into storage. Then, power can be sent ecstatically, or using pain, or with deep, mind-altering trance. There is no need to concentrate; the concentrated visualization is already contained in storage. Spare's magic addresses this. If the power is sent into the talisman through orgasm, for example, you can simply be in the moment, allowing the subconscious mind to do its work, confident that the meaning is contained in the "compressed alphabet" writing itself.

A lot of magical practitioners emphasize the momentum of power raising; indeed, the whole male/burst technique necessitates building and building in a (relatively) continuous stream, and that's the dominant technique nowadays. Two-step methods show us that power can be raised, saved, and *then* sent, and this is useful knowledge.

Mass Sending

There are times when large numbers of people, in a variety of locations, are raising and then sending power for a united purpose. This has been done in the magical community when the purpose was global, especially on a special occasion, or when the purpose has been timed to a political event, or when healing has been done on behalf of someone well-known around the world or around a region. I participated in such workings back when they were arranged via telephone—coordinating via the Web is obviously a good deal easier.

Coordinated Sending

In a coordinated sending, everyone agrees that their ritual will start at exactly the same time. This means *real* time—the purpose is for everyone to send together, so that if I am in New York I send at 9:00 p.m., and my friend in California sends at 6:00 p.m.

"Exact" time can actually be a bit tricky, especially if people have different magical practices. If my Wiccan tradition requires about ten to fifteen minutes of preliminary ritual before magic is performed, and your magical lodge requires twice that, then starting at the same time doesn't actually result in us sending energy at the same time. And as I've stated previously, working with timelessness is enhanced when there are no clocks or watches present in the ritual space, which can be an impediment to coordinating.

A mass sending need not be the work of hundreds of people. Two or three magical groups in two or three different locations might wish to sync up their efforts. Sending at close to the same exact time is easier with a smaller group, although pooling the largest amount of energy at the same time is more intense with a larger group. Basically, there will be some variation in the exact time of the sending, but it will cluster around the prearranged time like a bell curve: the more people involved, the more hits in the fat center of the bell.

I've used coordinated sending in much simpler circumstances. It can happen that a coven or other group is scheduled to meet and has important magical work to do, but one or more members can't make it. Maybe there's a blizzard. Maybe the car broke down. In this case, the group gets together and, as the ritual is about to begin, sends a message to those working solitary from home, and they are still "to-gether" magically.

Creating a Funnel

Here's a technique I used to help coordinate a large-scale working. In this case, Pagans, Witches, and magicians of all stripes were doing a coordinated working for a well-known Pagan who had fallen ill. There were literally hundreds of people all over North America (perhaps elsewhere) partici-pating. My then-husband had been one of the primary or-ganizers of the coordinated healing, and we worked at home with our coven.

We had a set time, but we knew that people would be sending energy plus or minus that time. We also knew that most people work in the male style, so that bursts of energy would continue to arrive over a period of time.

We decided on a female style of working, raising and sending in a long, slow, steady stream. We focused on visual-izing a huge funnel directly over our target's hospital. The purpose of that funnel was to receive and then direct the en-ergy, capturing it as it arrived and sending to the target. We used the slow wave of sending to maintain the funnel for a very long period of time, "catching" the energy throughout the period of the working.

Rolling Thunder

"Rolling thunder" is something I first learned about back in 2006, when the first coordinated mass workings began for Morning Glory Zell-Ravenheart, who had just been diag-nosed with cancer. (Morning Glory passed away in 2014.)

According to her husband, Oberon Zell-Ravenheart,

> It's coordinating a ritual not for simultaneity,
> but astronomically—such as at the local moment
> of a full moon according to each time zone.
> So, like a sunrise or sunset, it rolls around the planet.[20]

The idea is not to pinpoint an exact time and not try to co-ordinate the very large number of people who will be sending energy. Instead, let the power flow in waves to the target (such as to Morning Glory) as the earth turns. Since time zones "roll" across the planet with its rotation, allow the power to roll across Earth—hence "rolling thunder." In this way, a mass sending of energy can be organized without worrying about an exact time, and the target will receive a steady stream of energy over a period of time, rather than a single series of bursts.

Deciding How to Raise and Send Power

In the two chapters on raising power, we learned a wide variety of ways to do so, and in this chapter we focused on various ways to send that power, including the process of raising and sending. With all these methods to choose from, how do we decide what we're doing on any given occasion?

Practical Considerations

• What are the physical limitations of the participants? Are you asking those with mobility impairments to run or do the limbo? Are you asking someone with fine motor coordination problems to tie intricate knots or weave complex patterns?

---

20. Personal correspondence.

- What are the skills of the participants? Power raising via drumming requires someone who can keep a beat.
- What are the physical limitations of the space? Maybe there isn't enough room for the dance you've planned. Maybe rolling around on the ground is better in a carpeted space than on hardwood floors. Maybe lighting fires can't be done because you're in a fire-prone area in a drought.
- What are the privacy and noise considerations? Is a baby asleep in the next room? Have neighbors already complained about the howling after midnight?

Any of these considerations might guide your choices. A female/wave style of sending is often a way of working around physical limitations and noise restrictions, but there are many ways of quietly doing a male/burst sending or sending into storage. Members of a group who have differing levels of ability could be the cause for some creativity regarding splitting up duties. Suppose you've decided that walking a labyrinth to raise power and then sending at the center is the technique most suitable for your purpose, but one mobility-impaired member would struggle with that. That member could wait in the center, holding a clear visualization the whole time, increasing the power of the working. This is, essentially, no different from having the member with the best singing voice be the one to lead the chanting. We all have various abilities that can be used in magic, as well as weaknesses that sometimes must be worked around.

Timing Considerations

When raising power, one of the most important questions to ask is *What is the phase of the moon?* Moon-phase effects are among the most well documented and scientifically supported of magical concerns. Moon phase has a statistical impact on crime rates,[21] surgical outcomes,[22] fertility,[23] and more.

The waxing moon causes increase, while the waning moon causes decrease. The full moon provides the energy of fulfillment, sacredness, and lunacy, while the new moon brings energy related to darkness, secrecy, and mystery.

The flavor of the energy you raise should be consistent with the moon phase, so that you're not working against yourself—fighting the tide, if you will. The target and goal should also be appropriate to the moon phase.

From time to time, you will encounter an urgent need to send power during the "wrong" moon phase. Suppose, upon learning of Mondo's diagnosis and imminent surgery, it was just a few days after the full moon—it won't be a wax-

21. C. P. Thakur and Dilip Sharma, "Full Moon and Crime," *British Medical Journal* vol. 289 (December 22, 1984), 1789–1179, www.ncbi.nlm.nih.gov/pmc/articles/PMC1444800.

22. Robert Preidt, "Moon's Cycle Tied to Heart Surgery Outcomes: Study," *HealthDay* (July 22, 2013), https://consumer.healthday .com/cardiovascular-health-information-20/heart-stroke-related -stroke-353/moon-s-cycle-tied-to-heart-surgery-outcomes-study -678381.html.

23. Fiona MacRae, "Lunacy? Women Are More Fertile During a New Moon and Most Likely to Conceive During the Darkest Nights, Say Scientists," *DailyMail.com* (October 24, 2014), www.dailymail .co.uk/health/article-2807180/Women-fertile-new-moon-likely -conceive-darkest-nights-say-scientists.html.

ing moon for two weeks. So you'd use the diminishing energy of the waning moon to shrink Mondo's tumor instead of waiting for the energy of increase, which could increase the surgeon's skill.

Sometimes using the moon's energy involves making a simple linguistic change, reversing the phrasing from what we will create to what we will remove. We'll reduce risk, decrease pain, or unwind confusion, or we'll increase luck, improve health, or heighten clarity. Sometimes it's a more complex matter of reconceptualizing what the work actually is.

There are plenty of other timing considerations, including time of day, time of year, astrological and planetary influences, etc. The energy of planetary, zodiacal, seasonal, or cosmic events is present anyway and can't be avoided, so working with it simply makes sense. Allow these conditions to guide your power raising and sending choices.

In addition, you can choose to time non-urgent work based on the appropriate planetary timing. In other words, if you have magic that must be done on a particular day, then choose the energy techniques best suited to that day. But if you have work that can be done at any time, schedule it in accordance with planetary, lunar, or other influences. Even simple seasonal workings can help keep you in touch with nature and with your own life cycles, which is an added bonus.

Magical Considerations

Your primary magical considerations are the goal and the target. These should shape every decision you make about how to raise power and how to send power. Sometimes getting a handle on what that means energetically can be tricky.

There are many obvious correlations. A spell to improve one's ability to study should draw on mind skills for power raising. Any goal related to the home in which you live can send power into storage, since (a) it relates to storage/living/ having a space metaphorically, and (b) you can connect easily to the target by placing the talismanic object in your home. Fertility magic can be raised sexually and can use the meta- phor of male sending to replicate impregnation. As you think through your problem and your intention, you can come up with many creative ways of flavoring both the raising and the sending of power.

The Elements

When figuring out your intention and the appropriate flavor of the working, determining the elemental qualities of the work can be a powerful aid.

There are, indeed, many magical correspondences that can help your work. If you're a Kabbalist, for example, you'll be interested in what path or sephirah most closely connects to the work you're doing. A Pagan naturally is concerned with the gods or goddesses who have a relationship to the work. Tarot, astrology, runes, and many other disciplines can help to determine the flavor and style of a working.

I like to use the elements for a lot of reasons. In part, it's because they're simple (there's only four of them, five if you use spirit as an element) and yet almost infinitely complex. In part, it's because they're universal in Western magic. For instance, tarot, astrology, and Kabbalah all draw on the four elements, and roughly agree on the meaning of each.

What you're doing is figuring out the character and qual- ity of the energy you need by determining what element(s) should be present in the work. For example, is healing Mondo fire or water? Both elements correspond to healing. Fire is the life force, burning and awakening. Water is the gentle healer, compassion, love, and the embrace of wellness. Is Mondo strong enough to be able to take in fire energy? Is his tumor too aggressive to be treated with water? Asking elemental questions is a way of looking at the big picture.

If you've chosen to work with fire, this influences other decisions. Now you're likelier to choose a burst rather than a wave to send, and you can begin to set up your altar with fiery sympathetic objects.

I once taught a class on magic in which one of the attendees wanted to create a spell to find a new job. He had a strong earth focus to the spell he was constructing, which makes sense since earth corresponds to career as well as to money. But in listening to his actual goals, it was clear that he wanted a job that was more satisfying and fulfilling than the one he currently had. This wasn't about money but about feeling, and that shifted the work from earth to water. Naturally, a host of other decisions about how to raise and send power were quickly rethought.

eight

Spells

Throughout the previous chapters, we've mentioned spells, but we haven't really created any, or talked about what a spell consists of or how to devise one. Raising power is not a spell, and neither is sending power, although both of these are *components* of a spell.

As defined in chapter 1, **a spell is a series of steps taken to achieve a magical goal**. We've defined these steps broadly as: focus, connect, raise, send, finish.

Now we're going to fill in these steps with other necessary components and discover how spells become more intricate and specific.

"Spells" are often defined more strictly than the definition I'm offering. You will find magical practitioners who refer to spells only if something is "spelled out"—if there are magical words or magical writing used. By using a broader definition, I am encompassing a lot more of what you may consider to be a spell, and I am providing more options for your spellwork—that is, I'm saying, go ahead and construct your magical operation as suits your needs, and feel free to call it a spell regardless of whether or not it is "spelled."

Fine-Tuning a Spell

As you've been reading along, you've seen examples of spells or spell scenarios (such as healing our buddy Mondo), but we haven't executed a spell from beginning to end. It may occur to you at some point that raising power and sending power are actually pretty simple, and you may be wondering how spells get so complex.

First of all, spells don't *have* to be complicated. Simplicity is often a wonderful asset to bring to your magic, although complexity can be powerful as well. As in art, music, or cooking, both can have great appeal. In fact, I like to mix up how I do spells, because boredom is the enemy of staying focused and therefore of raising energy. So in my day-to-day practice, I'll use a variety of techniques, some simple and some complex.

Spells seem complicated when we look at all the necessary steps, but that's the danger of analyzing anything. Sentences seem complicated when you break them down grammatically, but "I am fine" is still a perfectly grammatical, and uncomplicated, sentence.

So let's not fear complexity, but let's examine the reasons that a spell is more than just sending power in a direction.

First, we are fine-tuning our understanding of both target and goal. As discussed in the previous chapter, this can require a lot of thought. A spell requires knowledge of how and where to focus; you need to know both what to focus on and what technique will impart the appropriate flavor.

Circumstances surrounding the spell should be examined. This includes the circumstances of the target, the conditions of the goal, and, of course, the circumstances of the magical practitioner. Here are some questions about these circumstances, the answers to which will contribute to fine-tuning a spell:

- What will it be like when the goal is achieved?
- Where is the target?
- How can I connect to the target?
- What are the physical, magical, and timing conditions?

Examining these circumstances will influence how to raise and send power. When you add power from natural or supernatural sources, or stored power, you'll be adding a variety of ingredients, and these contribute to the "window dressing" aspect of a spell. Power from herbs, crystals, and magical tools make a spell more complex to put together, but can also make it more powerful.

In addition, many of the bells and whistles of a spell come from creating a sympathetic connection. We talked in chapter 2 about "layering" connections. This could cause a spell to require a lot of ingredients. Use as many ingredients as feels right and are needed to establish a strong connection.

As you can see, the so-called complexity of spellcraft is actually the work of making a spell more specific and more powerful.

The Components of a Spell

Let's break down a spell into all of its parts and then go over the parts individually. Here are the components of a spell:

1. A stated goal

2. A target

3. Intention

4. Ingredients gathered beforehand (possibly none)

5. Raising power

6. Sending power to the target

7. Finishing the spell

The Goal

It seems obvious that a spell needs a clear goal, and indeed you may be thinking that it's hardly worth a mention. *Of course* you have a goal for your spell—otherwise, why do it at all? But in ten years of teaching classes on spell construction, I've found that the number-one stumbling block for people is figuring out what the real goal is, and getting specific about it. We have mostly used healing as an example throughout this book, because it is almost always the case that the goal in healing is unambiguous. In many other spells, this is not the case.

In chapter 7, I mentioned a job spell that changed from earth to water in its flavor. The earth spell was brought to my class on magic by the person who wanted the new job. Even though he was the one telling me that money mattered less than emotional satisfaction, he was also the one who created a money-oriented spell. In class, we worked on uncovering his true goal, and as this became clear, the entire construction of the spell shifted.

This is more typical than not, especially because a goal should be specific. When you want to achieve something magically, the first step of any spell should be to ask yourself a series of questions designed to uncover your true goal as clearly as possible. If this process leaves you thinking you're not ready to do a spell just yet, so be it.

When you start a spell, the first thing you should do is **state the goal out loud**.

Example 1: A Job Goal

- •What is the job I want? What's the job title? In what industry?
- •What is the salary range?
- •What is the commuting distance?
- •Do I want freelance or full-time work?
- •Are there other must-haves, such as medical benefits, a 401k, teamwork, solo work?
- •Are there dealbreakers, such as very long hours or working for the military, or other things that would make an otherwise perfect job unacceptable?

In this case, a resultant goal might be a full-time job as a systems analyst in the healthcare technology industry, paying at least $85k, with a full benefit package, within forty minutes from home, and with a company I consider ethical.

As you can see, examining this desire closely produces a much clearer goal than "a new job"!

Example 2: A Relationship Goal

- What do I want from a relationship? Am I looking for something now or for a lifetime? Do I want to marry the right person? Is marriage off the table?
- Do I want children with the right person? How many?
- Do I want a relationship that is monogamous or polyamorous or flexible?
- What gender is my ideal partner?
- What values must we have in common?
- Are there physical, cultural, and/or sexual must-haves?
- What are the dealbreakers?
- What are the things that feel really good in a relationship, that make me happy, that I hope to have?
- What are the things that make me feel bad in a relationship, that I hope not to have?

Notice that my relationship goals include must-haves and must-not-haves, and also include nice-to-haves and nice-to-not-haves. You're not negotiating a contract, where you only get the bottom-line stuff; you're doing magic, and you can ask for more than your rational mind believes you can get. It also doesn't have to be all serious and "meaningful." If you want a relationship with a Trekker, go ahead and add "Trekker" to your list.

Here, a goal might be this: The partner I will spend the rest of my life with, who laughs at my jokes, who thinks I'm sexy; a masculine, open-minded, liberal Pagan with a compassionate heart and a strong libido.

Note that you can leave things out if the answer to a question is "it doesn't matter to me." I'm a bisexual woman who prefers both men and women who are masculine-of-center, so "masculine" is an important word for me, but "man" or "woman" is not.

The Target

In the previous chapter, we learned that a target should be **specific, local, and informed**. I also stated, and it bears repeating, that the target is the single most important factor in determining the flavor of energy you will be raising and sending, and therefore it will start to shape how you raise, how you send, and all other steps of the spell. It's by understanding the target and goal that you will understand what the rest of your steps could or should be, and how to construct your spell.

Example 1: A Job Target

For the previous job goal, what's the target? There are a number of ways to work out a job spell target. If you have a specific company in mind, target the company—the hiring director or the physical location. Or target your résumé, making it attractive and compelling. In a pile of résumés (digital or physical), yours is the one that stands out. If your résumé gets responses but you struggle with interviews, then your target is yourself, and your goal is narrower: to be articulate, effective, and appealing in job interviews.

Example 2: A Relationship Target

For love spells, the target is usually yourself. A love spell can also take the form of a prayer—a request to God, a god, or your guardian angel to bring you and your "soul mate" together. In a spell of prayer, the target is the deity or your own higher self.

Both of these examples might toy with the idea of Fate, or what is "meant to be." This concept might be impossibly vague for you, and it might not even be something you believe in. On the other hand, it might be something you visualize clearly, a shining path through the universe. If this visualization is vivid and real for you, then it can be effective to use in targeting magic. Fate itself isn't the target; the target is pushing you and your goal together along the path so that, for example, you and your beloved inevitably meet on your fated love path, or you are drawn to apply for the right job, just as the right recruiter is drawn to you, on your fated career path.

Intention

In chapter 4, we defined intention as follows:

> *To intend is to focus fixedly and consciously on a firm desire, with determination and with absolute confidence.*

It's crucial to understand that *every* spell must be performed with a focused mind and firm intention. Often, you will read a spell in a book that doesn't say anything about "focus your mind"; you have to assume it. I've contributed to *Llewellyn's Witches' Spell-A-Day Almanac* a few times—spells are restricted to 150 words. Thus, I've omitted things like "ground and center," "focus your mind," "visualize your target," etc. You should always read any spell as if such phrases were included.

Intention means two things. First, it means that you are fully committed to the goal. Second, it means you focus your mind firmly on the goal during the course of the spell, as just defined (fixedly, consciously, etc.).

In almost every spell, splitting focus is necessary, as discussed in chapter 7. You must focus your mind firmly on the goal while also clearly imagining the target. The next step, gathering ingredients, is where you will determine if a focal object and/or an object of stored power can be used to represent one point of focus.

Examples

For both of the examples we've been working with, the job and the relationship, now is the time to review your goal and make sure you are really committed to it. Review the particulars of your goal, fine-tune the goal if necessary, and be able to fix it firmly in your mind.

Ingredients

There is perhaps nothing so associated with the idea of "magic spell" as the various ingredients a spell might contain. While it is true that you can do a spell without any ingredients at all, the "stuff" of a spell has a lot of value—in adding power, in creating a sympathetic connection, and in focusing the mind.

Collecting ingredients actually lends power to a spell, which I'll explain shortly. In addition, the process of slowing down and putting a spell together allows you to really consider what you are doing.

Magical Tools

Magical tools are a source of stored power, as described in chapter 6. Using them brings that power to your spell.

In addition, the power of preparing for ritual as an aid to focusing the mind cannot be discounted. The use of magical tools serves as a trigger to induce the appropriate state of mind. This is an effect that will become apparent over time. Obviously, the first time you use a tool, you will not have the trigger in place from repetition. What you *will* have, though, is the knowledge that this tool is associated with magic, and the psychology of working with something laden with archetypal power will serve your purpose.

Preparing your ritual space, setting up the working area, putting on magical garb or jewelry (or disrobing if you work skyclad), and assembling and then using tools all help to lead the mind into the proper state for focused intention, while also bringing stored power to the work.

Power Objects

Objects that have inherent power are obviously of great use in spells. I keep reference books in the house to help me figure out the appropriate herbs, stones, colors, numbers, and so on to use in magic. You may be thinking, "Reference books? Why not use the Internet?" But often there is as much wrong "information" online as there are reliable resources, particularly in the occult, so a well-worn favorite volume is my go-to (see appendix C).

Virtually every spell I use will have the four elements on the altar, so the minimum, for me, will be to select incense (which I'll be using anyway) that is appropriate to the occasion.

Sympathetic Objects

You already know that creating a sympathetic connection is vital to the success of a spell. Sympathetic objects can create many connections—to the goal, to the target, to ideas inherent in the magic—and naturally you needn't choose just one of these. For example, if you are doing magic to help a couple, you can have a sympathetic object for each person.

Sympathetic objects can be symbolic or direct.

Direct: Photos, mementos, directly connected objects (nail or hair clippings of a targeted person or animal) or indirectly connected objects (soil from the path of a targeted person)

Symbolic: Colors, elements, runes, astrological symbols, tarot cards, abstract ideas (a pen representing inspired writing, a rattle representing babies, etc.)

Collecting Ingredients

One of the first things my teacher told me was that a spell might start working even before you do it, but that you had to follow through and perform the spell or else the effect would dissipate. So if you're planning to do that love spell, you might suddenly get a spate of first dates, or if you're preparing to do the job spell, you might start getting interviews. But if you don't proceed to actually perform the spell, you won't get the second date or the second interview (or you will, but not the end goal—the job or the long-term relation-ship).

Eventually I came to understand why this "pre-spell" ef-fect was occurring. Partly, of course, spells transcend time, so the linear order of "before the spell," then "the spell," then "after the spell" gets a little screwy. But a lot of it has to do with planning the spell and gathering its ingredients.

As you plan and gather, you'll be thinking about, focus-ing on, meditating on, mulling over, and visualizing the spell. You can't help but do so! Suppose a spell calls for cinnamon and a green candle. You go to the supermarket and find the cinnamon, but they have only white and red candles, so you make a second stop for the candle. The entire time you're out and about, you're thinking about the spell. While find-ing your ingredients, you're thinking about how you will use them. While standing in line at the store, you recall that cinnamon draws money, and that relates to your goal. While driving from the supermarket to the candle store, you think about how green is also associated with money, and you picture lighting the green candle. You imagine the shade of green you will select (you hope the store has that shade!), so your thoughts are suffused with green and drawing money.

It is primarily the power of your focused mind that cre-ates the pre-spell effect. Follow-through is vital, though. Consider that if you don't do the spell, that fact will remain in the back of your mind. It will feel, perhaps, like a failure, or an incompletion, and the energy of your prior focus will dissolve. Also consider that the energy of preparing for the spell had the quality of reaching toward something, and the "something" was the performance of the spell. Without follow-through, that energy will fall flat, as if the target was removed while the arrow was mid-flight.

So even if you actually get the job offer or meet "the one" before you actually do the spell, be sure to go ahead and do the spell.

A Magical Chest

Naturally, you'll end up with a stock of spell ingredients you use often. You will not always have the luxury of carefully planning a spell. If you get an emergency phone call that so-and-so was in an accident and needs energy *right now* (and I've had several of those phone calls over the years), you should have what you need at hand (or enough to improvise). In chapter 10 you will find a list of basic ingredients to keep on hand that will allow you to do almost any magic on the fly.

You'll acquire additional ingredients because you won't use everything up in a single spell. Herbs and oils in particular are bought, grown, or made in quantities larger than any one spell will consume, so you'll have leftovers. In addition, it's probably smart to buy extra quantities of ingredients you need. When you're at the store getting your green candle, get a few. Candles (especially tapers) have an unfortunate tendency to crack on the way home, so you don't want to buy just one, and since green was useful once, it may come up again, so buying for a rainy day is a good idea.

Eventually, you'll end up with a magical storage chest, closet, or shelf. Now, here's a cool thing about that: The magical chest will, itself, become an object of accumulated power. Every time you do a spell, you go to your magical chest, with your mind on your work. Whenever you're in that state of mind, buzzing with focused energy, you're there, putting something away or taking something out. Eventually, the act of opening the magical chest will be one of the ritual steps that gives you power.

Example 1: Ingredients for a Job Spell

You have a goal and a target. Now it's time to devise the actual spell.

Since your target is your résumé, the first ingredient you need is a printed copy of your résumé. Keep in mind that this is a sympathetic object—it isn't necessarily the one you will send out. In fact, if you're going to anoint and cense it, it shouldn't be, since you don't want to send a résumé with water stains and the scent of incense. Rather, "That which is like a thing *is* the thing." A printed copy of your résumé is like all other printed and electronic copies, and the magic you do on this one printout affects them all.

The two most common spells throughout history are to bring love and to bring money, so you'll have a wide selection of incense ingredients to choose from. Since (in this example) you are looking for a job in the healthcare industry, you can add healing herbs to your mix and perhaps something associated with your planetary ruler as well.

I'm a Taurus, a sign ruled by Venus, so I might choose mugwort, plumeria, rose, or some other Venus ingredient, plus cinnamon to draw money, or vetivert, which is both ruled by Venus and associated with money. Cinnamon also has associations with being on a higher spiritual plane, which is great because I'm looking for a company with high ethical standards. I might add marjoram for healing and happiness.

You might have a batch of incense you use on a regular basis—I do. In that case, you can take some of it, mix in your extra ingredients that are specific to this spell, and voilà! Shortcut to spell-specific incense!

Green is the color of money and career, so that would be a good color for a candle or candles and for my altar cloth.

What spell am I actually *doing,* though? These ingredients could be generic to almost any spell. As I look, I notice a lot of my ingredients are kind of watery and soft—healing and Venus both bring a kind of sweetness, as well as the element of water, to things. Thinking it over, I realize I need more fire in my spell. Fire is intense and passionate. I want go-getter energy and the quality of strong attraction. I also want the element of earth, which is associated with career, stability, and money. I decide to use fire during the spell and earth at the finishing stage.

A simple way to bring fire into a spell is to burn something. I will need a cauldron, dish, or container large enough to hold two pieces of flaming paper (my résumé) without getting out of control. The container should be resting on a ceramic tile so it doesn't burn the altar cloth or floor. I also need a fire extinguisher nearby just in case.

Here are the ingredients for my job spell:

- Résumé
- Green candle
- Green cloth
- Matches/lighter
- Cinnamon, marjoram, vetivert
- Cauldron and tile

- Fire extinguisher
- Censor and charcoal

Example 2: Ingredients for a Love Spell

I am targeting myself in this spell.[17] The idea is to become an attractant to the kind of love, and the kind of loving partner, I'm seeking. There are lots of ways to do this, but one method is a magical bath.

Love is associated with the element of water. I want to suffuse myself with a particular kind of attraction, so "soaking in it" can work both metaphorically and literally—joining the metaphor to the literal is an effective magical technique that I use often.

In the previous example, we used the planet Venus because it is the planetary ruler of my astrological sign (Taurus). Now we can use Venus again, because she is the planetary ruler of love. In astrology, the number of Venus is six, but in the Kabbalah, the planet Venus is associated with Netzach, which is the seventh sephirah. For this reason, the spell can utilize either six or seven candles, depending upon which association you're using. Let's assume we're using six.

Pink is associated with love, and red is associated with passion. In my goal, I identified "strong libido" as part of what I'm looking for, so I want to include both colors.

Many plants attract love, including rose, patchouli, jasmine, gardenia, and rosemary. Plants and oils that incite lust include clove, musk, cinnamon, hibiscus, patchouli, and

---

17. In fact, I have both a good job and a happy marriage, so I'm not performing either of these spells for myself. But let's use me as our fictional subject anyway. I've performed similar spells in the past.

rosemary. Some of these can go into the bath as herbs or oils, and some can be burned as incense.

I want to maintain the idea of surrounding myself with love through the end of the spell, so wrapping myself up in love after I get out of the bath feels powerful. A new pink towel or bathrobe, never before used (you'll find this called "virgin" in old spellbooks), will allow me to step from my love bath into more love.

Here are the ingredients for my love spell:

- Sea salt
- Six candles: three pink, three red
- Censor and charcoal
- Matches/lighter
- Pink and red rose petals
- Vanilla and patchouli oils
- Incense, including cinnamon, rose, and jasmine
- A new pink towel or bathrobe

Raising Power

Where in your spell are the sources of power, and how will you access them?

At a minimum, every spell *must* have:

- Power from the mind through concentration and focus (visualizing the target and goal)

Almost every spell has:

- Power of repetition and power of suggestion through going through steps, using tools and objects that are familiar and associated with magic

Any spell *can* have:

- Power of deity, gained by evoking or petitioning the deity or deities as a preliminary step
- Supernatural power from evoking or petitioning other supernatural beings
- Stored power from using magical tools
- Natural power from using incense or aromas, and potentially from using other natural objects on the altar
- Supernatural power from the four elements, by balancing a spell in the elements as a preliminary step or from one or two elements specifically needed by the spell

Why would an evocation or petition to deity be a preliminary step? In part, this is out of respect for the entity summoned. If God or a god is called upon, it is polite to honor that deity by placing him/her/them at the head of the line. In part, it's practical. You can pray to a deity at the end and say, "Bless what I have done here," but if you pray to a deity at the beginning, saying, "Bless what I am about to do here," then you (theoretically) have the deity's attention throughout the spell. It's kind of like saying, "Hey, watch this."

In addition to these, you can add other power sources to your spell. Will you chant? Play the drum? Dance? Use meditation and deep trance? Weave? Use sex or pain? Go out in nature? Use barbarous words? Or meaningful words? Will you act out your goal, using imitative magic? Every spell is different. Your power should come from a source that has an appropriate flavor.

Example 1: Raising Power for a Job Spell

As with every spell, I will raise power in this spell from my mind, by concentrating on my target and goal. I recommend starting every spell with a stated intention, which will add the power of words immediately. By having the spell include some speaking, I can use the power of meaningful words. They help create the intention of the spell, while raising additional mental power.

One technique I like very much—an age-old magical technique—is to repeat a simple phrase over and over. The idea is to reduce your intention to a word or two, and repeat that as a chant, an incantation, or in writing. In this case, I've decided to chant or intone my intended job title, which is two words. This uses rhythm and repetition as well as language.

I can easily access stored power from one or more magical tools. An athame to direct my will seems an obvious choice. Perhaps I'll be able to add items to my altar that I've used before, which have accumulated power from use.

I'm going to burn incense, and the qualities of the herbs and spices I burn are a natural source of power. I can also add power from the four elements (a supernatural source). It makes sense to balance this spell, because a good job uses all the elemental qualities: air for intelligence, fire for energy and passion, water for a job I love, and earth for money and stability. I often start spells by charging up symbols of the four elements for balance and to bring this power to the spell. Since I'm consecrating the résumé, the elements should be present anyway, to use during that step.

I'm going to bring the résumé to the four elements, charging it with the power of each. This raises more power from the elements, flavors the spell, and brings repetition to the spell. Any time the elements are used, there's an ability to use repetition. For example, look at these words to charge my résumé with the elements:

I do charge this résumé with air, that it capture the thoughts of those who read it. O air, O communicator, let this résumé be a powerful messenger, bringing swift communication from the employer I seek.

I do charge this résumé with fire, that it be a force of my True Will, awakening and enlivening the employer who reads it.

I do charge this résumé with water, that it open the heart of the employer I seek, that deep satisfaction be a part of my work.

I do charge this résumé with earth, that it bring stability and prosperity. O earth, make this new job a home for me!

Because "I do charge this résumé with (element), that it" is repeated four times, it has a sing-song quality that alters consciousness. This is a technique I almost always use.

Any spell can include power from deity, by opening with an evocation or prayer. In this case, I've chosen to evoke the Roman god Mercury. He is often used nowadays as a god of digital technology—computers, wireless communication, telephony, and so on. He's also generally a god of swift communication, and I want to hear back quickly from a prospective employer.

I'll flavor the power with a sympathetic object—the résumé—and with color—the green of the candles and altar cloth. The deity I've chosen to evoke also flavors the power. Of course, by using the job title as a magic phrase, I cannot avoid imbuing the power with the flavor of the job!

I've also decided to burn the résumé to bring more fire to the spell, and to bury its ashes to seal the spell with earth, and these are part of flavoring it.

Example 2: Raising Power for a Love Spell

Flavoring a love spell is very important. Every part of it has to feel romantic and beautiful and be oriented toward love. Unless you want an asexual relationship, the spell should feel sexy as well. In this example, I've chosen myself as a target, so my state of mind is especially important. It's not enough to concentrate on my target and goal; I have to *feel* romantic, I have to *become* and *embody* romance. So I will design a spell with a heavy emphasis on atmosphere. I'll make everything lovely, in soft, romantic colors. I'll use flower petals and sweet smells to beautify the experience. This raises power in a psychological sense, by concentrating the mind on love, but the primary purpose is symbolic and sympathetic.

As with the job spell, this spell raises power from the mind through concentration and meditation, and power from words through stated intention. Because I want to call someone to me, I'm choosing words in this spell that are meaningful, connecting again to the mind and heart as the beloved is described in the spell. This will be part of creating the atmosphere, so I'll want my words to be beautiful and appealing.

I almost always use an athame or wand in my spells, accessing stored power from a magical tool, and I'll do so here as well.

This spell can easily use the power of deity, for a number of reasons. First, because finding your true love or soulmate is something seen as spiritual, as tied up with your Fate (capital F!) or life's purpose. Thus, God, your guardian angel, or some specific deity can be thought to be interested. Second, there are many deities who rule over love, including the goddesses Aphrodite, Ishtar, Áine, Freya, and Erzulie and the gods Kama and Eros, so it can be fitting to evoke them in a spell where they can be expected to want to lend energy. Finally, in this particular spell I've stated as my goal a "Pagan" partner, so evoking gods we might worship together would be appropriate.

This spell relies heavily on natural and supernatural power. Flowers, oils, and incense are natural, and the balance of the four elements is considered supernatural. Since I'm using the element of water as a bath, the elements won't be perfectly balanced: water will be disproportionately present. But I want a long-term relationship, so I want something that also has air, fire, and earth qualities, as all lasting relationships will have all four.

Once I decided to use six candles, I went down the road of numerology and will repeat six as a motif in the spell. Numerology can be considered a supernatural power source as well as a source of symbolic sympathy.

A love spell has a target that naturally works with sex magic, so let's add that to the sources of power in this spell. Orgasm is one of the greatest means of accessing the body's power. Since this spell will be done alone, in the privacy of a bath, and since it is meant to draw a relationship that is, in part, sexual, it's a perfect fit.

Sending Power to the Target

As our "male" and "female" metaphors emphasized, sending power to the target is the climax of the spell. Often, a spell has a bunch of steps, and it is easy to get caught up in the ex-ecution of these steps. So it's important to understand a kind of through-current of energy from beginning to end. No matter what the steps are, how simple or how complex, no matter whether you're using a spell from a book, one you've written yourself, or one you created spontaneously, on the fly, there is always a stream of energy. From the moment you first begin to focus your mind, that energy builds, full of the flavor and imagery of the goal. It builds and builds until it is finally released toward the target. Building the energy is like pulling your arm back in archery: ultimately you let go and let the arrow fly.

We've described a number of different ways to raise and send power:

- In a burst (male)
- In waves (female)
- With split focus, either with a partner, with a group, or solo (the sending can then be burst or wave)
- Into storage for later release
- As a coordinated working among many people in dis-parate locations

When creating a spell, choose your method based on prac-ticality (like how many people are present, how much noise can be tolerated, how long the ritual should last, etc.) and on matching the style and flavor to the purpose of the spell. If you are sending out an urgent call for justice, then a gentle series of waves is a bad match—a burst is a more urgent energy. On the other hand, some healings demand gentle energy that can be tolerated by a frail patient. Political magic can be forceful, like a boisterous protest march, or gentle, like persuasion and influence. Consider the intent and the way you want your energy to manifest.

Example 1: Sending Power in a Job Spell

Looking at the components of the spell I've put together, I find that the energy is building through preliminary steps: the charging of the elements, the evocation of the god Mercury, and the charging of the résumé. My concentration and focus increase with each step, as more and more power is brought to bear.

At this point in creating the spell, I ask myself, how can I push this power out, in a burst, to the target (my résumé)? It seems, looking at the spell components I've put together so far, that the whole thing is kind of quiet. With the candle, the four elements, and a sympathetic object, I can put together a decent spell, but I want more. I want some *oomph*. While thinking about this, I came up with the idea of chanting the job title. Since I'd previously thought of burning the résumé to bring extra fire into the spell, burning it at a peak of power seemed like the ideal way to send power. Raise and chant, raise and chant, and at peak, set the document on fire. Mentally and emotionally push the energy through the document, through the fire, up through the smoke and out into the world, where it can do its work, borne on the smoke.

Example 2: Sending Power in a Love Spell

This love spell is a perfect example of how preparing for the spell can be part of the power-raising. All this beautification and preparation feels like an anointing of the self, bringing love in. From the time you first clean the bathroom, to bringing in the flowers and the pink towel, to the first declaration of intent, everything seems to move me toward receiving love, until I get into the bath and I'm soaking in it, literally and magically.

How, then, do I prevent the bath from kind of fizzling out? After all that build-up, how do I make sure that simply sitting in a tub, focusing, receiving, stays powerful?

There are a number of options, including singing, meditating, gazing at the candles, etc. I'll probably start with that, but I'm choosing to culminate this spell with an orgasm. Again, since I've specified that I want a lot of libido energy in my lover, this is a great way to summon that energy, and orgasm naturally flows to peak-and-release. A lot of time, people lose mental focus during or leading up to orgasm, so I have to make sure I fully meditate on and absorb the idea of myself as a target, drawing a lover to me, before beginning the sexual part of the spell.

Finishing the Spell

Many people think that a spell is finished when the power is sent to the target. Mostly it is, but what happens next is important. After you finish a meal, clearing the plates is different from lingering over a cup of good coffee. After sex, throwing your clothes on quickly is different from cuddling. After you fill your tank, screwing the gas cap back on is important. Finishing matters.

Declared Success

The first thing to know about finishing a spell is this: **Always declare success**. This is the seal on the mental focus you've given the spell. As soon as you remove yourself from the mindset of the spell, doubt may begin to appear. Perhaps it's doubt about the result or about your skill as a practitioner of magic, or maybe it's skepticism about magic and the occult arts as a whole. These doubts are the natural activities of an intelligent mind, but it's easy to see how they can undermine your work. Therefore, as soon as you are done, declare success. It is the final use of focused clarity during the course of the spell. Your subconscious mind will hear that declaration while you are in an altered state, and it will have a powerful impact.

Phrases such as "So mote it be," "So be it," or "It is done" are often used to finish a spell for exactly this purpose.

Often, when working in a group, nothing more is needed at this point. We exchange glances or nods, affirming that the work is complete, and then declare success. Immediately, we ground.

Grounding Out

When you ground and center at the beginning of the working, you are bringing your energy into a still place that is connected to the earth. At the end, though, you are doing something that is also called "grounding" but is a little different. You are again connecting to the earth, but this time you are doing so in order to release residual energy and come back to yourself. This is also known as "grounding out," "grounding down," or "earthing" the energy. A useful phrase here might be "Come down to Earth."

When I complete a ritual, I touch or slap the floor or ground and/or stomp my feet. It brings me back to my day-to-day self in a hurry, and it feels great. Sometimes, though, I'm in a Wiccan ritual of which a spell is just a part. The spell is done, but the ritual will continue. In this case, I will do something quieter and less disruptive. Physical contact is often very grounding in this way. In a group, holding hands or hugging after a spell is done is effective. Touching the ground or the floor is good. Eating and/or drinking is not only a great technique but often is necessary after a spell—magic works up an appetite!

In the typical Wiccan rituals I have at home, I consecrate cakes and wine and then do any works of magic afterward.[18] Even though we've symbolically partaken of the consecrated food and drink, I ask participants to avoid eating until after the magical work is completed.

Food, especially, tends to go a long way toward making you feel earthbound. That's helpful at the end of a working, when it's time to ground out, but beforehand it makes your job harder. You should feel light, able to travel in the imagination (if not the astral), when working magic. There's a dual advantage to saving the cakes and wine until after magic, though: when magic is done, we're invariably ravenous!

The Remains

Many spells leave something behind, and a spell isn't truly finished until you've figured out what you're doing with that.

I will never forget the first conversation I had with my teacher on this subject. She was explaining poppet magic to me, and I asked what happened to the poppet when you were done. She said, "Oh, you put it in a shoebox under your bed.

---

18. A detailed examination of Wiccan ritual, the order of the steps, and the reasoning behind them, including cakes and wine, can be found in my book *The Elements of Ritual*.

And eventually you have a bed with lots of shoeboxes underneath."

So, that's no good. Seriously, my teacher was fantastic, but I knew right away that I didn't want the rest of my life to include an ever-growing pile of shoeboxes. So I started thinking about what gets done with the remains of spells, what *could* get done with them, and what it all meant.

There are usually remains from the four elements. Consecrated water should be poured out onto the earth or into natural water; dumping it in the sink or toilet is inelegant and maybe a little disrespectful to the whole idea of consecration. If you've created saltwater in the course of your ritual, be careful not to pour a large quantity of it onto living plants. Ashes from incense can be taken outside as well. If you burn incense in a censer, tamp down the ashes and place the next charcoal, next time, right on top. Salt and incense can simply be reused.

Then there are the ingredients specific to the spell.

The easiest spell to discuss here is the one with no remains. A simple candle spell burns the evidence, so to speak. The candle is burned all the way down, and there is nothing left. If the incense has been consecrated specifically for the spell (as opposed to consecrating it as a representation of air), then just consecrate a small amount and burn all of that as well.

Other spells create talismans, tokens, or other objects meant to be kept, to keep the spell working. Some such talismans are kept indefinitely. For example, a dreamcatcher might be hung over the bed; you'd keep such an item more or less forever. A protective item (such as a dreamcatcher) can be recharged periodically, but its usefulness remains. A protective talisman for a car or a home, for example, can be cleaned and recharged when you get a new car or move to a new home.

There are a vast array of spell ingredients, though, that don't need to be kept forever—at least not in order to fulfill the purpose of the spell—and aren't self-disposing like a candle. For these, some thought should go into how the remains are to be handled.

Offerings can be made from the remains of a spell. For example, you can do a money spell using coins as sympathetic objects. At the end of the spell, the coins could be given to charity. Spell remains can be placed upon the earth, provided they're not pollutants or litter. This can symbolize offering them to the gods or to Mother Earth or setting them free.

Burial does a number of different things, depending upon the intention. It can stabilize a spell, allowing its energy to partake of earth elemental energy; a spell is made strong and permanent by being made a part of the earth.

Similarly, many spells take advantage of the idea of the land, and buried spell ingredients are "planted" like seeds or placed into the ground like a foundation. The Catholic tradition of burying a Saint Joseph statue in order to sell a house partakes of this; the saint is made a part of the piece of real estate. A protection spell for a piece of property or a home often involves burying something on the property; the protective power becomes part of the land.

Burial can also allow the energy of a spell to dissipate slowly. This is applicable when you want to achieve a long-term goal. Suppose, for example, you did a spell to maintain a high GPA in college. Since the spell has to continue working for four (or more) years, you might choose to make burying a talisman a part of the spell.

To put something into the earth can also be to hide it, to make it secret. The concept of earth as a dark and secret place is leveraged. This can be anything from burying a real secret, to something working on an "out of sight, out of mind" principle, to a trap laid for an enemy.

Finally, to bury something can be to put it to rest, to kill it off. Here, burial as in a funeral is the imagery being used.

The specific use of burial is invoked by whatever is said during the process or, if silent, by the concentrated thought behind the act. Location also makes a difference in burial. Burying something on your own property has a different connotation than burying something in a remote woods, which is itself different from burying something in a churchyard or at the edge of a cemetery.

Burning also has different meanings under different circumstances. To start with, it imparts fire energy, and thus passion, will, and intensity can be brought to bear.

Burning something can be seen as distilling it into its purest, noncorporeal form. In the job spell, for example, we turn the résumé into *all* résumés, into the quintessence of "résumé." Burning also allows something to travel throughout the world, or to the heavens, carried on the rising smoke. So you can write down something you wish to come to pass and burn it, sending the message to God or the gods, to your guardian angel, or simply out into the universe where it can become manifest.

Fire can also be the means of an offering. Some ancient pagan cultures—such as Hellenistic Greece—treated a burnt offering as that which sent the essence of a thing to the gods. Gods cannot eat actual meat, for example, but their burnt essence is consumed. This was done in the Greek ritual of *thysia*; the inedible portions of the sacrificed animal were burnt and offered to the gods, while the humans feasted on the rest of the meat. It was not just the burnt portion that was an offering, though, but the burning itself; the fire transformed inedible meat into something fit to offer the gods. Conveniently, this leaves the physical meat for the worshippers to consume thereafter.

Burning can also be treated as negative. Fire devours and destroys. People write down things they wish to be removed from their lives and then burn up the paper.

The ashes that remain after you burn something are usually considered to be waste and don't have to be disposed of ritually. However, they *can* be used ritually—buried or scattered—in order to finish a spell.

Running water can be used to purify or release the remains of a spell. Obviously, if you're using a natural stream to dispose of a spell's remains, you should be conscious of not polluting. The elemental quality of water used is usually purification, but there's also a sense of travel, which is why running water is often specified in old spells. The item used in a spell is released to go *somewhere*. By contrast, if an item was dropped into a lake, it would pretty much always be in that lake. Dropping something (non-polluting) into a lake might have a quality similar to burial, in that the object is hidden away.

Exposure can use the air to scatter something or leave its fate to God or the gods. Something is left on the ground to let the wind, or birds, or just entropy scatter it wherever it will go. Again, be conscious of pollution and litter if you use this technique.

The Rule of Silence

The rule of silence is something discussed in many books on magic and by many teachers. It has a range of variations. The basic principle is this: Don't talk about a spell after you've done it. The variations go like this: Don't *ever* talk about a spell after you've done it, or don't talk about it *until its goal is accomplished* (or until it has been proven to fail[19]), or *for the next twenty-four hours*, or *for a full cycle of the moon* (that is, until the moon returns to the phase it was in when the spell was performed). You get the picture.

What is the purpose of this rule?

My teacher likened talking about a spell to throwing a baseball and then plucking it out of the air to see how fast it was going. However fast it *was* going, it isn't going that fast anymore, and by your interference you've ensured it will never reach its intended target.

---

19. By "proven to fail," I mean, for example: You did a spell for a specific job for which you interviewed, and you've received a call from the recruiter that someone else got the job. You did a healing and the patient died. You did a fertility spell for a woman and she tells you she's having a total hysterectomy, thus ending the possibility of her becoming pregnant. Or, you did a spell with a time limit built in, such as "XYZ will happen by the next full moon." The time limit has passed and XYZ didn't happen. Even if XYZ might still happen, the time limit means the spell has "expired."

It's important to let the energy go, to release it from the confines of your conscious mind. To devote any thought to it is to impede the flow of that release. Naturally, you will sometimes think about it, but you can more easily set those thoughts aside if you know you will definitely not speak about it. The minute you speak about it, any doubts you have (about the potential results or about how well you performed the spell) will unavoidably creep back in.

You have been working on your mind skills, but you're not actively applying them all day, every day. There are times when you are relaxed, when you are goofing off. By putting the spell out of your mind and not engaging with it, you avoid having your thoughts poke around at the spell when they're not being actively disciplined.

Let it go.

Constructing a Spell

How do you go about constructing a spell?

First, figure out what the problem is. Determining the goal and target is almost always the hardest part. You start with a problem: someone needs a job, someone is sick, someone wants a career change, a life change, a new baby, a good verdict in court. There are thousands of potential issues that inspire spellcraft. Work with the issue to figure out as much about it as possible. Don't be afraid to use your intuition to help you through parts of the problem that start out a little fuzzy.

Start thinking about what that goal and that problem *feel* like. Maybe you think the subject needs more structure, more discipline, to achieve the goal. In that case, a highly structured spell might be in order. Maybe the subject needs to assert more self-control. In that case, perhaps you shouldn't do a spell on behalf of the subject as a third-party—he or she needs to participate. Or maybe you feel like there's a really simple solution, but you just don't know what it is. Make sure simplicity informs the spell itself—too many elaborate steps would be counterproductive.

Brainstorming

In my coven, we have brainstorming sessions before any spell. First, we determine if we will do the spell at all. We discuss the ethics, the practicality, and how we can make a connection between ourselves and the target. Often, we change the concept of the spell entirely.

How can we help a very sick child whose mother refuses to bring her to the doctor? One possibility is to do the spell to heal her directly, but that doesn't address the issue with the mother. In one particular case, we were dealing with a child with a chronic illness, so there was a risk that we might heal an occurrence but not the entire illness—ideally, the mother would be willing to monitor the illness later on down the road.

Magic also works best when mundane and magical efforts are combined—we wouldn't work healing magic for an adult who refused to see the doctor. Is our example of helping the sick child the same? Is it ethical to try to change the mother's mind? What about sending her a dream? The mother was traumatized by the circumstances of her husband's death—could that be keeping her from doctors? What about sending a comforting image—a doctor's visit that feels safe? If we send an image in one of these ways, is that ethical, since she still is making up her own mind?

How can we help a couple in the middle of a divorce when we have love and friendship for each of them? If we send energy to help one, does that somehow harm the other? What's the right energy to send to both of them? "Fairness" was rejected as sounding like a measuring and divvying-up; that kind of thing can be emotionally damaging. "Peace" was rejected for the opposite reason, as it might lead to feelings of surrender and *un*fairness. What about "best possible outcome"? Is that too vague? If it's vague but as close as we can get, is it worth doing the magic?

How can we help a person whose request to us is for a job, but whose job seeking is impaired by issues with clinical depression? Do we do one working or two? If one, do we work on the job or the depression? Can we combine the two goals, or does that dissipate the power of the spell? What about "positive energy for effective job seeking" as a goal? What about "personal breakthrough that leads to a new job"?

Choosing a goal helps us choose the target. In the last example, if "personal breakthrough" is chosen as a goal, then the target is obviously the job seeker himself.

In each of these cases (all based loosely on real-life examples), choosing the goal and the target helped us begin to understand the flavor of the energy, and therefore exactly what the spell would be.

For healing, I keep anatomy books in the house. Being able to visualize the exact part of the body being targeted is very helpful. The Internet is always available as well, for definitions of illnesses, for geography, and so on.

At this point, we start to talk about the energy in a fairly specific way. For example, for a friend with a cardiac condition, we pinpointed blood flow as a crucial issue and began to think about ways to create smooth and successful flow. Eventually we developed a spell wherein water was poured from one container to the next, flowing smoothly, building the energy of the spell while it imbued "flow" into the energy we would eventually send. For a depressed person who really wasn't facing reality, we started talking about the idea of movement and eventually began walking around the circle. The walk was imitative magic for the person, who needed to *walk his path* and who needed steady movement out of his difficulties.

At the same time, we're figuring out who will concentrate on what (with a group, most participants concentrate on the goal while one concentrates on, and sends to, the target), what ingredients to use, and what will be on the altar. For a woman with fertility issues, we wanted something small on the altar so we could send it to her immediately. During a more complicated working, we charged a piece of jewelry. For another fertility spell, we used an egg.[20]

---

20. Like most people, I have friends and family who don't all know each other. At my wedding, it was delightful for people in my magical group to finally meet two of the babies they'd helped bring about through fertility magic.

Exercise 19: Develop a Goal and Target

Now is the time to start thinking about your own magical goal(s).

Begin mapping out the questions to ask yourself. Be as specific as possible. If you don't have answers yet, that's fine; formulating the questions is a great start. Think about the specific questions for a goal offered in the examples in chapter 8 (for the job goal and the relationship goal), and also think about what that goal feels like, which we just discussed.

Does your goal suggest a target? If not, start imagining what your target might be. If a target seems impossible to find, go back to the goal—is it specific enough? A vague goal will make finding the target more difficult.

First Steps

I have described more than one step that could or should be first in constructing a spell. At various points, I've recommended grounding and centering, stating the intention of the spell, and evoking a deity (if you use that step) as first or preliminary. What order should these steps actually be in?

First: Ground and Center

Readying your mind must always be first, because without your mind being in the proper state, none of the rest of the steps can be truly effective.

You will be doing various preparations, such as getting out your magical tools or setting up your altar, and your mind will begin to center itself around these activities. Once you're ready to formally begin, ground and center again to bring yourself fully into the moment. In a group, ground and center once you're all in place together.

If you (alone or in a group) are doing a spell as part of a larger ritual—at a certain point in a Wiccan circle, for example—then it's ideal to begin the ritual with grounding and centering. Then briefly re-center when it's time to do the spell.

Second: Declare Your Intention

This step completes the process of grounding and centering and formally begins the spell. It's like grounding and centering is saying "I am here," and declaring the goal is completing the sentence with "in order to (achieve this goal)." A stated intention can be the purpose of the spell—for example, in the sample job spell in the next section, "I will have a full-time job … with a company I consider ethical" is the stated intention. Or it can be much simpler, such as "Tonight I work magic," with your detailed goal fleshed out elsewhere in the spellwork. Everything you do will be sharpened by having that stated intention behind it.

I like to state my intention out loud, whether working solitary or in a group, because words have a particular power that just thinking to oneself does not.

Third: Elemental Balance (Optional)

If you are balancing the spell in the four elements, the power of that balance should be accessible to everything else that happens. Subsequent steps will have more power and completeness with the elements already present, and you can, on a purely practical level, use those elements in whatever is done next, such as charging a sympathetic object.

This step is not about consecrating a ritual or sympathetic object by the elements, but is simply a matter of bringing the elements present to the space. You'll see an example of these steps in this order in the sample job spell in the next section.

Fourth: Prayer, Evocation, or Petition of a Deity (Optional)

If you do both steps 3 and 4 (balance and pray), then I would balance first. To do so creates a kind of elemental temple for the deity to enter. It prepares the mind, the heart, and the space you're in to receive the presence of deity.

All of these are "getting ready" steps, and whatever spell you do can be preceded by them and should have at least the first two built in.

The Sample Spells

Here are the two spells—the job spell and the love spell—that we've used as examples throughout this chapter and chapter 8. As we go through the spells, I'll point out on the side things we've learned in this book and how they are used in each spell.

The Job Spell

Please note that this spell and the one that follows use the language from the examples in chapter 8. If you use the spell, you'll obviously change the goal and job title to suit your own needs, just as you will change the qualities of a romantic partner to those uniquely suited to you.

Set up the altar with a green cloth and green candle. On the altar are:	Green creates *symbolic sympathy* with money/career goals.
Censer with charcoal Incense Matches/lighter Small cauldron or dish on a tile Water Salt Athame Résumé	Component 4 of a spell: ingredients gathered beforehand Component 2 of a spell: a target (the résumé)
Light the candle.	
Concentrating on your goal, say:	Component 3 of a spell: intention
I will have a full-time job as a systems analyst in the healthcare technology industry, paying at least $85k, with a full benefit package, within forty minutes from home, and with a company I consider ethical.	Component 1 of a spell: a stated goal (that is specific)
Place your athame in the dish of incense, saying: *I do charge you with the power of air, power of the mind, of intelligence, and of movement. So be it!*	Component 5 of a spell: raising power Power is being raised from: • Repetition (repeated phrase)

Place your athame on the (lit) charcoal, saying:

> *I do charge you with the power of fire, power of the will, of passion, and of purpose. So be it!*

Add incense to the censer and inhale the smoke.

Place your athame in the water dish, saying:

> *I do charge you with the power of water, power of the heart, of empathy, and of kindness. So be it!*

Place your athame in the dish of salt, saying:

> *I do charge you with the power of earth, power of the body, of stability, and of finance. So be it!*

Add salt to the water and stir.

- Natural sources (incense ingredients)
- Supernatural sources (the elements)
- Stored power in a magical tool (the athame)
- Magic words

Evocation to Mercury:

Component 5 of a spell: raising power

Intelligent and bright, swift and scientific, Bright lord Mercury, ruler of digital technology, Mighty one, Hear my prayer: Lend your power to this work. Look upon my goal and see it is worthy. Give to me your aid in achieving my ends. Thank you.

Power is being raised from:
- **Deity (by evocation and by offering)**

Add additional cinnamon to the censer, saying:

Accept this offering of cinnamon, O Lord Mercury, in thanks for your aid.

Lift up the résumé, saying:

Component 5 of a spell: raising power

Résumé! Foot in the door! Shine brightly in the eyes of all who read you! Bring attraction! Bring interest! Let employers look upon you and be inspired! Let them read you and want to meet me and hire me!

Power is being raised from:
- **Magical words**
- **Supernatural source (elements)**

Pass the résumé through the smoke, back and forth, so that it is thoroughly censed, saying:

*I do charge this résumé
with air, that it capture the
thoughts of those who read
it. O Air, O communicator,
let this résumé be a powerful messenger, bringing
swift communication from
the employer I seek.*

*I do charge this résumé
with fire, that it be a force
of my True Will, awaken-
ing and enlivening the
employer who reads it.
So be it!*

Now sprinkle the résumé
with saltwater, thoroughly,
getting both sides. Be sure
especially to touch your
name and desired job title.
(Don't *soak* the paper—
you're going to burn it.)
Say:

*I do charge this résumé
with water, that it open
the heart of the employer
I seek, that deep satisfaction be a part of my work.*

*I do charge this résumé
with earth, that it bring
stability and prosperity. O
earth, make this new job a
home for me!
So be it!*

Concentrate on the résumé while visualizing your goal. Begin chanting your desired job title slowly, over and over, while you fold the paper in half and then in half again. (You want it small enough to fit into the cauldron, but not so tiny that it won't easily ignite.)

Say:

Systems analyst! (fold)

Systems analyst! (fold)

Find a rhythm to the job title, *SYS-tems-AN-a-LYST!* and chant it like a beat. Clap your hands in tempo to the chant, gradually gaining speed as your intensity builds.

Component 5 of a spell: raising power

Power is being raised from:
- **Concentration (the mind)**
- **Rhythm**
- **Magic words**

When you're ready, pick up the paper and light it in the flame of the candle, then drop it into the cauldron. As you watch it burn, visualize the flame taking it out into the world, sending its message magically just as you will send other copies of it physically and/or digitally.

Component 6 of a spell: sending power to the target

Remain at your altar, watching the flame until it has fully burned out.	
You can allow the candle to burn down completely. After the flame is out and the ashes have cooled (it can be the next day, if you wish), take the ashes outside and bury them, saying: *My new job is in the earth, steady and strong like the earth, stable and long-lasting like the earth. So be it.*	**Component 7 of a spell: finish the spell** **• Disposition of remains** **• Declared success**

The Love Spell

Clean the entire bathroom so it is spotless. Move the ordinary things (toothpaste, hairbrush) so they're not visible. Make sure only fresh, clean, unused towels and washcloths are present. Have your new pink bathrobe or towel in its place.

Beautify the bathroom however it feels right to you. Beauty is an important part of any love spell—make sure the room is pleasing to you. It should look, feel, and smell lovely. You can play recorded music that is romantic or beautiful as well. Flowers are a great idea—you will be using rose petals, so a vase of roses can be a part of the space too.

You are working with six as a magical number. Rewrite your goal so that it contains exactly six or twelve qualities for your ideal partner. Your flowers should be a multiple of six as well.

Create an altar in your bathroom on a small table, at the sink, on the floor—whatever works with the space. The altar should contain:

- Sea salt
- Six candles: three pink, three red (unlit)
- Censer and charcoal
- Matches/lighter
- Pink and red rose petals
- Vanilla and patchouli essential oils, or a blend of the two
- Incense, including cinnamon, rose, and jasmine
- Your athame or wand (I'll say "athame" throughout the spell, but use whichever is comfortable for you.)
- A representation of Aphrodite

The altar, too, should be beautiful. You should be pleased by the layout, by the dishes in which things are held, by the candleholders—all of it.

Component 4 of a spell: ingredients gathered beforehand

Symbolic sympathy:
- **The colors pink and red**
- **Beauty (associated with love and romance)**
- **Numerology (numerology can also be considered a source of supernatural power)**

Fill the bathtub to a comfortable temperature. (You'll find that salts and oils blend with bathwater best when they are added as the tub is just filling, rather than at the end. If you prefer, fill the tub partway now and add the rest of the water after the other ingredients are added.)

Place the six candles, alternating pink and red, around the outside of the tub. Don't light them yet.

Declare your intention. Earlier, I created the following goal:	**Component 1 of a spell: a stated goal**

> *To find the partner I will spend the rest of my life with, who laughs at my jokes, who thinks I'm sexy; a masculine, open-minded, liberal Pagan with a compassionate heart and a strong libido.*

We're going to build the description into the actual spell, so for now simply state:	**Component 3 of a spell: intention**

> *I do a spell of love.*

Place your athame in the dish of incense and say: *O air, open my mind to those around me, that my beloved comes to me.* Light the charcoal in the censer. Place your athame on the lit charcoal and say: *O fire, ignite my passions, that my beloved comes to me.* Place your athame in the bathtub and say: *O water, imbue me with loving attraction, that my beloved comes to me.* Place your athame in the dish of salt and say: *O earth, strengthen my commitment, that my beloved comes to me.*	**Component 5 of a spell: raising power** **Power is being raised from:** • Repetition (repeated phrase) • Natural sources (incense ingredients) • Supernatural sources (the elements) • Stored power in a magical tool (the athame) • Magic words
Take some of the flower petals and/or a flower, and place them at the feet of the Aphrodite image. Focus on her beauty and her loving nature. Say:	**Component 5 of a spell: raising power**

Aphrodite, lady of love, I call to you. *Be here, in this place of beauty and love.* *Be here for me, as I open my heart to your blessings.* *Be here to bring two of your worshippers together.* *I invoke the gracious one,* *The beautiful one,* *The delightful one.* *Look upon the work I do,* *blessed Aphrodite,* *And aid me.* *I thank you.* *Blessed be.*	**Power is being raised from:** • **Deity (by evocation and by offering)**
To make my stated goal work for this spell, I converted the qualities to six lines. I then added a call at the beginning and end.	**Component 1 of a spell: a stated goal** **Component 3 of a spell: intention** **Component 5 of a spell: raising power**

I call my beloved! *I call my masculine life* *partner.* *I call a compassionate* *heart and an open mind.* *I call the one who finds* *me sexy and wants sex* *often.* *I call someone who laughs* *at my jokes.* *I call someone liberal.* *I call a Pagan partner.* *I call my beloved!*	Power is being raised from: • Magic words • Supernatural source (numerology)
Light the candles. With each pink candle, say:	Sympathetic connection to the beloved
For love, for love, for love. *My beloved comes to me.*	Sympathetic use of color
With each red candle, say:	Component 5 of a spell: raising power
For passion, for passion, *for passion. My beloved* *comes to me.*	Power is being raised from: • Magic words • Repetition
Take the incense and wave it over the water. Say:	Component 5 of a spell: raising power
I call my beloved. I am *attractive to my beloved.* *My beloved comes to me.*	Power is being raised from: • Magic words • Repetition
Add six pinches of sea salt to the water. Say:	• Supernatural sources (the elements, numerology)

I call my beloved. I am attractive to my beloved. My beloved comes to me.

Add six drops of your oil(s) or, for a stronger scent, a multiple of six (twelve or eighteen should be plenty). Say:

I call my beloved. I am attractive to my beloved. My beloved comes to me.

Sprinkle the rose petals over the surface of the water. Say:

I call my beloved. I am attractive to my beloved. My beloved comes to me.

• Natural sources (the oils)

As you step into the tub, clearly visualize yourself being surrounded by, bathed in, and changed by the magic you have created. See the soft, pink light of love surrounding you, calling to your unknown partner like a beacon.

Component 2 of a spell: a target (yourself, surrounded by love, being a beacon of love)

Bathe in this pink and passionate light, visualizing it growing in intensity.

Component 5 of a spell: raising power

Power is being raised from:
• **Concentration**
• **Visualization**

Bring yourself to orgasm in the bath, sending the power of your climax into your spell.	**Component 5 of a spell: raising power** **Power is being raised from:** **• Sex** **Component 6 of a spell: sending power**
When you are ready, step out of the bath and wrap yourself in your new pink towel or robe, saying: *It is done.* Allow the candles to burn out completely. Enjoy the flowers while they're fresh, then leave them, with the flower petals, in a remote place as an offering to Aphrodite.	**Component 7 of a spell: finish the spell** **• Disposition of remains** **• Declared success**

Exercise 20: Construct a Spell

In exercise 19 you came up with a target and goal. Now it's time to put together the steps you've learned so far to create your own spell.

What ideas, flavors, and energies will you create? What is the through-energy of the spell?

The ingredients list is something you can come up with after you've written the entire spell, but thinking about ingredients can be inspiring and help you create the spell. Answer these questions:

• What elements are associated with your spell?

• What color(s) could be a part of your spell?

• What herbs could be associated with your spell?

• What numbers could be associated with your spell?

How will you raise power and how will you send it? Answer the following questions:

• Are you working alone, with a partner, or in a group?

• Will your target respond to gentle energy or forceful energy?

• What flavor do you want to impart to your spell?

• What methods of raising and sending power are fun for you? (Pleasure is a *huge* asset to magic.)

How will you finish the spell?

Bag of Tricks

In this chapter we'll go over a bunch of useful tips and tricks for creating magic, including instructions for how to do the preliminary and integral spell steps mentioned in this book—consecrations and evocations. Simple spell structures that can be applied to any situation are also here, as well as some of the spells mentioned in the body of the text. There's also a list of basic magical supplies that are useful to keep around.

Stocking Your Magical Shelf

It's worth discussing the ins and outs of buying magical supplies. After considering details of certain purchases, you'll find a shopping list of basics to keep in the house so you are prepared to do just about any spell. Obviously, this list can be expanded. Of course, shopping for supplies lends energy to a spell, and it's by no means necessary to have everything on hand before you begin spellwork. But there are times when a spell might be urgent, or when you're performing a spell after stores are closed, or when you change direction in your spell planning at the last minute. It's certainly convenient to have a basic stock at home.

Candles

Candles require a little discussion because there are so many different kinds and they have different uses.

- Tapers (often sold as "dinner tapers") are a magical basic, because they are sturdy enough to be lightly carved, they are accessible to be dressed (see the section later in this chapter for how to dress a candle), and they come in every imaginable color. They burn for about eight hours, which is convenient for any spell where "keeping watch overnight" is a motif.

- Votives are the short, squat candles. They also come in a huge range of colors, although many are scented, which can run counter to the needs of a spell. They can be carved, but their short stature limits the surface area. Because of their larger base (compared to a taper), they sit sturdily, even without a candle holder, so they're good for any spell where you're burning a candle on top of a magical object such as a jar. They burn for about four hours.

- Seven-day candles are the ones that come in the pillar-type glass holders. Keep in mind that there are two kinds—the wax can be poured directly into the jar, or the candle can be formed and then inserted into the jar. If you want to dress, carve, or in any way manipulate the candle, then the poured kind is useless. In either case, the jar makes these candles really handy for outdoor rituals because the flame is kept out of the wind. They're also ideal for any spell that lasts for a period of days. They're safe on virtually any level surface, provided you protect against anything that might knock a candle over—animals, toddlers, earthquakes, etc. Color availability is okay—you can get a basic assortment of primary colors, and they're almost never scented (which I appreciate!). As the name indicates, they burn for about a week, but it depends on how they're made. I've had them last for only four days, and they can burn as long as eight or nine days.

• Many other candle types are nice for extra light, for marking an area (such as a circle or even a labyrinth) with light, or for creating atmosphere, but are less useful as focal objects in spells. Tealights, for example, are small, are not often removable from their little tin cups, and burn down quickly. They're nice for surrounding an area with candlelight, but are not my choice for focal objects. Pillar candles come in thousands of shapes, sizes, and varieties. They might have glitter or crystals and are often scented. They may burn for weeks. I find a pillar is nice for long-term dedication. My Brigid candle (dedicated to the goddess Brigid and burned periodically in her honor) is a large pillar.

- White candles can be used for virtually any spell or ritual purpose. Other colors have more specific purposes, but if you have a limited budget and are going to buy only a few candles, buy white. When I'm out and about and spot candles of a color that I don't have or that might be hard to find, I buy them for my supply chest. You never know when a sky-blue candle will be called for, after all!

- Since you're burning candles and incense, always have a small fire extinguisher nearby.

Incense and Herbs

Almost every mention of incense in this book assumes you're burning loose incense on a charcoal. The advantages of this are myriad, the most important of which is that you can easily make your own custom blends. I also like that you can increase and decrease the level of smoke at various points. So you can burn incense at the start of your ritual, allow it to dwindle, and then throw a pinch on the censer when it's time to consecrate something using incense smoke. By contrast, sticks and cones burn steadily until they burn out entirely.

I use stick incense when I want to "set it and forget it"— for example, when I'm meditating. I also keep stick incense around as a backup in case of charcoal failure. There was an incident several years ago when I bought a package of defective charcoals, and every time I lit one, it exploded. This wasn't quite as dramatic as it sounds, but it was certainly inconvenient. More commonly, charcoal can get damp and refuse to light. I store my charcoals, which come wrapped in foil, in a zipper bag in the freezer to keep it dry.

I like smudge as well, but it's limited: There are only a few things you can smudge with—usually sage, cedar, or sweet grass. The very nature of smudge—wrapping the herbs in a bundle—means you can't use ingredients that don't lend themselves to that shape, such as resins or flower petals. The bundles also don't stay lit, so you light one for the moment of use and then put it down, where it'll go out quickly, making it inconvenient any time you want steady smoke.

Smudging has specific ritual purposes, mostly having to do with purification, and spells of other types can call for incenses of other types. Smudging is also specific to certain Native American cultures, so people who are concerned with cultural appropriation might not be comfortable with it.

I smudge when the need arises, but my go-to incense is a loose blend on a charcoal.

When using a charcoal in a censer, place the charcoal on a bed of sand, earth, or clean kitty litter in the censer. After the first time you do this, you'll have ash blended with your original bed thereafter. Use a censer that has a handle that dissipates heat—you want to be able to lift it without burning your hands. (Many spells don't call for carrying the incense, but some do.)

In my home I always have a sage bundle, a package of stick incense, and some loose frankincense. Frankincense burns easily because it's a resin. For the same reason, it's a good addition to many incense blends and helps bind them together. It's useful in a wide variety of spells because it purifies, consecrates, raises the vibrational level, and brings luck. As with sage, purification isn't a part of *every* spell, but it can blend with other, more targeted herbs. For a love spell, for example, you might pass a focal object through the smoke of a frankincense and rose blend—frankincense for consecration and rose for love.

If you keep only one fresh herb, it should be rosemary. First of all, it's a great culinary herb and is fantastic in a wide variety of recipes. Keep fresh rosemary for your kitchen, and as it gets old, allow it to dry for incense. Both fresh and dried rosemary, both leaves and stems, are useful in magic. The scent of rosemary is evocative and has both magical and physical aromatherapy functions. There's now some scientific evidence that inhaling rosemary improves the memory—something Witches have been saying for hundreds of years.

Rosemary is something of a universal substitute. It can be substituted for frankincense in many spells, but it has even more uses. Rosemary is good for purification, concentration, mental powers generally, luck, love, and lust.

Fabrics and Cords

Fabric is handy for a number of spell purposes. A simple mojo bag has many uses and is made from a square of fabric. Altar cloths in colors appropriate to the working can layer symbolism onto a spell. You can combine a writing spell with a textile spell by writing on fabric—either using embroidery or other stitchery, or with fabric paint or magic markers. Objects can "wear" colors for magical purposes—the only limit is your imagination.

Magical objects—perhaps something created or consecrated within the course of working a spell—can be wrapped in fabric as a final step before carrying, burying, hiding, etc. Black fabric is said to be ideal for this purpose, as it is a kind of barrier to vibrational energy. Some people keep their athame and/or wand wrapped in black—often black silk—to preserve the energy, and so as not to absorb symbolic energy from any other color.

White fabric is the opposite: it can absorb any energy and is excellent for absorbing the energy of other colors added to it, such as with thread, paint, or magic marker.

I find it handy to keep a simple black silk (or silky nylon) scarf around in case something needs to be wrapped up. For some reason, this is the kind of thing that seems to come up at the last minute. Maybe in the course of brainstorming a spell right before executing it, we decide to add an object to be carried or whatever, and I have all the other spell ingredients but didn't prepare for that one. So keeping the black silk around works for me.

I also find a coarse white cotton to be a handy possession. Not only can it be dyed or painted when any other color is needed, but it can also be used as a cheesecloth, for draining herbal mixtures and pressing herbal oils.

A spell might call for thread, string, or yarn. If you're actually sewing, you need thread, and if you're actually embroidering, then embroidery silk is ideal. Otherwise, anything from a fine thread to a coarse twine to clothesline might work for some purposes. In most cases, you'll want to pick up the thread for the individual spell as part of getting that spell together—keeping a supply of threads, yarns, and strings in your home is probably not practical unless you're really into textile arts, textile magic, or both.

If you're going to keep a little something around, a ball of red yarn is practical. Red is the color of life and life's blood, of lust and passion. It can be added to many magical workings to add life energy to the work, and when a tie or connection is symbolized by some kind of string, red yarn makes that connection visually alive and vital.

Oils

The most frequent magical use of an oil is to infuse it with an herb or other substance. The infused oil can then be used for anointing a person or object, dressing a candle, or otherwise creating sympathy.

In other words, impart a quality to the oil, and then whatever you put the oil onto partakes of that quality. The quality can be derived from consecration or charging, or from herbs or other substances. The quality can be anything: love, sacredness, success, peace, victory... The list is as endless as your magic requires.

For this reason, you want to use an oil that doesn't have a strong scent of its own and can easily take on the qualities of the infusion.

Typically, extra-virgin olive oil is perfect for such uses. It's handy, too, because you probably also use it in the kitchen.

Any vegetable oil will go bad eventually, so if you're keeping oil just for magic, use one with a long shelf life, like jojoba.

Other

- You'll probably want symbols to represent the four elements. (See the lists of elemental correspondences in appendix A.)
- It's a good idea to have a couple of clear quartz crystals around. I'm always finding these in gift shops for very

little money. Clear quartz can be used to represent spirit if you work with five elements rather than four. Clear quartz can also absorb almost any magical energy, so it can be a token, memento, or talismanic object for a variety of spells.

• Consider getting a set of small dishes—like finger bowls. You can use them to hold various symbols on the altar (water, salt, incense, etc.). I've often needed an extra one for a spell and was glad that I really love little bowls and always seem to have a nice one around.

A Magical Shopping List

• Candles: white tapers and white votives to start, then add other colors as available and affordable

• Lighter, matches

• A small fire extinguisher

• Fresh rosemary

• Frankincense

• Charcoals and censor

• Incense sticks and burner

• Black silk scarf

• White cotton fabric

• Red yarn

• Olive and/or jojoba oil

• Sea salt

• Dishes

• Elemental symbols

• Clear quartz crystals

Consecrations

Knowing how to write a good consecration is a skill that will be used time and time again in your magical life. You'll consecrate the elements, you'll create sacred space, you'll charge sympathetic objects, you'll send power into talismans. You'll use this skill *all the time.*

Here's what a consecration should include:

1. What you're doing

2. Specification of the thing being consecrated

3. How you're doing it

4. What it accomplishes; what you want from it

5. Declaration of success

Ideally, the consecration should also sound good and be relatively simple.

Here's a simple consecration of anointing oil:

By my True Will I do charge and consecrate this holy oil,
that it may bless all those touched by it. So be it.

What just happened?

By my True Will	#3 (**How**)
I do charge and consecrate	#1 (**What**)
this holy oil,	#2 (**Specification**)
that it may bless all those touched by it.	#4 (**What it accomplishes**)
So be it.	#5 (**Declaration of success**)

You can change the tone or feeling of the words, making them more or less formal, making them rhyme, or whatever you like. The important part is these five simple elements that allow your intent to manifest effectively.

If you ask God, or a god or goddess, or another supernatural being, to aid in this consecration, then the request is the "how"—the implication is that it's by the power of the being. If you simply say "I charge you" or the like, you're implying it's by your own will, by your own power, by the strength of your words, that the work is being accomplished. You must *know* what you're implying, in either case, so that the intent is there.

Here is another example of a consecration:

> *Gracious Mother Goddess, bless this salt,*
> *bringing the power of earth to my ritual. Thank you.*

This is even simpler than the first one, but it does the trick:

Gracious Mother Goddess,	#3 (How)
bless this	#1 (What)
salt,	#2 (Specification)
bringing the power of earth to my ritual.	#4 (What it accomplishes)
Thank you.	#5 (Declaration of success)

Let's look at how the résumé was charged in the previous chapter:

> *Résumé! Foot in the door! Shine brightly in the eyes of all who read you! Bring attraction! Bring interest! Let employers look upon you and be inspired! Let them read you and want to meet me and hire me!*

Résumé!	#3 (How) It doesn't say "I" or evoke a deity here. Because you are *commanding* the résumé—using the imperative—the implication is that the power enters from your will and word.
Résumé! Foot in the door!	#2 (Specification) The word "résumé" is literal, while the phrase "foot in the door" is metaphorical; both say what is being charged.
Shine brightly in the eyes of all who read you! Bring attraction!	#1 (What) The imperative also is a way of saying what you're doing. Instead of saying "I charge you to bring attraction," you use a command that brings both the "I" and the "charge."
Shine brightly in the eyes of all who read you! Bring attraction! Bring interest! Let employers look upon you and be inspired! Let them read you and want to meet me and hire me!	#4 (What it accomplishes)

So be it!	#5 (Declaration of success) This is said at the end of the group of consecrations— the résumé is charged first, then it's consecrated by the power of the elements, then you say "so be it." Since the multiple consecrations are all part of the same spell, you don't want to cap off any one of the consecrations, finishing that piece of the energy flow, before completing the set.

Language

It's almost a shame that every consecration, evocation, and spell in this book sounds like it was written by me. Since I'm the author, there's no avoiding it. But that doesn't mean my style of writing is the "correct" style for magical language, which is why I try to change it around.

When you perform a consecration, consider the different mood and feeling of the following:

- Third person: *I consecrate this salt of earth*
- Second person: *I consecrate you, O salt of earth*
- Imperative: *Be consecrated, salt of earth!*
- Formality versus informality
- Brevity versus detail
- Archaic versus modern language (*thee* and *thou* versus *you*)

- Spoken versus sung words
- Rhyme versus prose language

Exercise 21: Consecrations

Write a set of consecrations for the four elements. They can be as simple or as ornate as you like.

After completing your consecrations, try making changes to them as just described in the "Language" section. If you wrote in third person, create a version in second person. If you wrote a simple, brief consecration, try adding more description, etc. Say the consecrations out loud. If you trip over your tongue on a word or phrase, consider replacing it.

Do you like what you've written? Use your consecrations in ritual. Do they sound good? Do they feel powerful?

Evocations/Invocations

As discussed in chapter 5, an evocation—calling upon a deity or supernatural being—has also got some basic necessary components. It's similar in structure to a consecration.

Magic doesn't require that you evoke or invoke any deity. However, if you do, I think you want to, and should, do so with reverence. It is perhaps pointless to evoke without honor and reverence, and it is probably unwise.

Remember, these are the components of an evocation:

1. An invitation or summons
2. Specificity in words and atmosphere
3. Descriptiveness
4. Praise
5. Need or reason
6. Greeting and/or thanks

The greeting and/or thanks is a declaration of success. Once you have invited Mother Goddess, "success" is that she has arrived, and you greet her and/or thank her for coming.

Although there is no "how" here—you don't necessarily have any particular power to call God or a god—you can draw upon a relationship with the deity as a reason they should listen to you. For example, "I, who make offerings to you daily, do call you" is a powerful thing to say (if it's true). The power here is devotion. Or you can draw upon a similarity or affinity, pointing out to Brigid, goddess of poets, that you are a poet, or to Bast, goddess of nurses, that you are a nurse. Finally, your "how" can be an inducement in the need or reason component. The reason is analogous to "what it accomplishes" in a consecration, but it can also motivate the deity. A healing god can be told, hey, this is your thing.

Here's the Aphrodite evocation from the sample love spell in the previous chapter, and how it breaks down according to our components:

Aphrodite, lady of love,	#2 (Specificity)
I call to you. *Be here, in this place of beauty and love.*	#1 (Invitation/summons) The invitation repeats in every "be here."
Be here for me, as I open my heart to your blessings. *Be here to bring two of your worshippers together.*	#1 (Invitation/summons) #2 (Specificity) This begins to create a specific atmosphere. #4 (Need/reason) This has a bit of the "how" described previously—an open heart attracts Aphrodite, the purpose of bringing two people together attracts her, and her worshippers attract her.
I invoke the gracious one, *The beautiful one,* *The delightful one.*	#3 (Descriptiveness) #4 (Praise)
Look upon the work I do, *blessed Aphrodite,* *And aid me.*	#5 (Need/reason)
I thank you. *Blessed be.*	#6 (Greeting)

How to Dress a Candle

Since dressing a candle has been mentioned several times, it's worth providing some instructions.

Technically, "dressing" is applying oil to a candle. There are other things you can do to prepare a candle prior to using it in a spell. Often, a candle is engraved with a knife or pin. People do a lot of other really creative things with candles, like using glitter, embedding crystals, and so on. Some of these things work fine with oil, and some make a mess.

The simplest way to dress a candle is to take a pure oil (olive and jojoba were mentioned previously, but other oils can be used) and apply it to the candle from the center down and clockwise, then from the center up and clockwise, all while concentrating on your intention.

You can complicate this a little by infusing the oil with herbs or other substances sympathetic to your purpose.

You can also charge or consecrate the oil prior to applying it to the candle.

That's all there is to it! Use this step before any candle spell to add additional power to the work.

All-Purpose Spells

I love being creative with my spells, changing them up and adding imaginative touches that connect me deeply to my target and goal. The variation is something that keeps my mind focused, since I'm easily bored. But it's also useful to know basic spell steps that can be used for virtually any purpose.

Here is a simple candle spell to be performed solitary, and a simple group working. These spells can be doctored up with additional steps, sympathetic objects or qualities, or imitative behaviors, or they can be used pretty much as is (although you'll need to plug in the things unique to your spell in any case). They can form the basis of highly individual spells. Go back to the job spell in the previous chapter and you'll see that the core of the solitary candle spell is contained within it but a lot more was added.

Any spell can have an added step of prayer or evocation, but these steps are omitted in the following pages because this is a book about spells that can work with any kind of spirituality. You can pray to God, evoke your personal god or goddess or guardian angel, or proceed as outlined, without calling upon any higher power. You can add a step for prayer or evocation as described in chapter 9.

A Solitary Candle Spell

1. Set up an altar with a candle, the four elements, and a sympathetic object representing your target. The candle should be of a color associated with your target or goal, and the incense should likewise have ingredients associated with your target or goal.

2. Ground and center.

3. Declare your intention.

4. While reciting the goal, dress the candle with an oil infusion also associated with your target or goal.

5. Light the candle and the incense.

6. Consecrate the sympathetic object by the four elements.

7. Gaze into the candle, visualizing the goal while sending power into the target/object, which is before you or in your hands.

8. Declare success.

9. Let the candle burn all the way out.

Here's a trick I like to use with this spell: use a dinner taper as your candle. Do the spell just before bed, and leave the candle burning in a safe location in your bedroom. (Always have a fire extinguisher nearby just in case!) Dinner tapers burn for about eight hours. This means the candle will burn through the night. I find that a candle burning in my room all night will tend to hover around the edges of my consciousness, almost but not quite waking me, and infiltrating my dreams. It doesn't make for the soundest night's sleep, and I don't do it often, but having a spell work its way through my dream state is powerful.

A Group Intonation Spell

1. Before you begin, think about your intention, and decide on one or two words that encapsulate it. For example, a love spell could simply be "love" or "true love" or "soulmate."

2. Set up an altar with the four elements, plus a sympathetic object representing your target. The incense should have ingredients associated with your target or goal.

3. Ground, center, and merge.

4. Declare your intention.

5. Consecrate the sympathetic object by the four elements.

6. Have one person (the person most deeply connected to the target or goal) sit at the altar, holding or gazing at the sympathetic object.

7. The group members now join hands. The person at the altar can join hands with the group or remain

apart in the center. You can all figure out what feels most comfortable and powerful.

8. Intone your one- or two-word intention. You don't all have to tone together. You can allow your voices to blend, to harmonize, to weave around one another, to rise above and below one another. You can create rhythms with the word(s).

9. As the power builds, allow your hands to gradually rise so that, at peak, the group's hands are all raised in the air.

10. Send the power to the target.

11. Declare success.

Here's what chanting "love" might be like:

Person 1	*Loooooooooooooooove*
Person 2	*Love! Love! Love! Love!*
Person 3	*L O V E L O V E L O V E*
Person 4	*LlllloooooOOOvellllllloooooOOOvvvve*

I'm sure you're impressed with my musical notation! I imagine Person 1 doing a long, single tone, like an "om," while Person 2 is saying the word forcefully, like a drumbeat. Person 3 is using a deep, bass, repeated tone, and Person 4 is singing the word up and down the scales. None of them are doing the same thing, but they're all merged in intention and purpose, and their energies naturally play off one another. It's likely that, by the end, they're all together.

Some Spells Mentioned in This Book

Throughout these pages, I've mentioned a number of spells in passing. Now that you've completed a course of instruction in how to perform spells (by which I mean, now that you've read the previous chapters), you're ready to execute any of them. Here are a few to get you started.

These spells should give you creative options. Reading "A Spell to Reunite Lovers" should teach you more than a spell to reunite lovers! By reviewing the following spells, you should gain an understanding of how to use candle movement (and other object movement) in a spell, how to use braiding as a textile magic technique, how to use a poppet in magic, and how to create and use a talisman for a long-term goal.

A Spell to Reunite Lovers

This spell is used to bring together two people who have had a falling out. The title of the spell uses the word "lovers," but it can be a romantic couple (married or not), a friendship, or family members. Some people might consider this a spell that interferes with the free will of the individuals, but I think there are circumstances where it's appropriate. If two people aren't speaking, or one left abruptly without explanation, and neither is abusive, then this is an appropriate spell. Even if they reunite only long enough to have a heart-to-heart talk so they can end their relationship more peaceably, that's a better outcome.

I once performed this spell for a couple who had lived together for years. When "Joe" moved out, he described himself as depressed and confused. "Paul" was heartbroken. It sounded to me like *neither* wanted to be apart, so the spell seemed appropriate. After I completed the spell, Joe came home, and the two were happy together for another five or six years. When they parted, they did so as friends, which they remain to this day.

This spell will use the names Paul and Joe as examples.

Perform this spell during a waxing moon. It will be performed daily for seven days. You can end on or before the full moon.

1. Get two candles, one in the color of each person's astrological sign (see the list of astrological correspondences in appendix A). You can also engrave each person's name into his or her candle.

2. Set up an altar with the candles about two feet apart from each other (figure 7). About halfway between them but forward (there should be nothing exactly between the candles), place one or more symbols of love and harmony. I have a rose quartz crystal in the shape of a heart that is perfect for a spell like this. The incense should likewise be halfway between the candles but behind (see illustration). The incense should have ingredients associated with love and harmony. A candle snuffer can be off to the side.

Figure 7: Altar Setup

3. Ground and center.

4. Declare your intention: *Joe and Paul will be reunited.*

5. Dress the candles with oil scented appropriately. Use rose or gardenia for love, lemon for friendship, or basil for harmony in general. As you dress Joe's candle, say, *This is Joe.* As you dress Paul's candle, say, *This is Paul.*

6. Light the incense and meditate on Joe and Paul. Visualize them clearly. Inhale the scent of the incense and feel harmony and love permeate your work.

7. Light each candle, again saying, *This is _____.*

8. Say, *Joe and Paul, now apart, are moving closer together.*

9. Move each candle about an inch closer to the other. Meditate and send power into the candles.

10. When you're ready, say, *Joe and Paul are closer*, then snuff the candles.

11. Repeat this spell every night for seven nights.

12. On the seventh night, change step 8 so that you say, *Joe and Paul are now together.* In step 9, when you move the candles, they should touch.

13. On the seventh night, end with *It is done! So be it!* Let the candles burn all the way out.

A Fertility Braid

Create a braid to be worn by someone wishing to become pregnant. For this spell, you don't need to be at an altar. You may wish to be at your usual working space for magic, or you may wish to be someplace where it's a little easier to manipulate the braid. Personally, my solitary magical altar is on a dresser, and I stand when working spells. For this spell, which takes a pretty long time, I sit, with the ends of the yarn or cord anchored securely.

This spell should be done during a waxing or full moon. I didn't put a time limit on this spell (such as "Jane will be pregnant within a month") because this is a spell that can be shared. In other words, once the woman wearing the braid becomes pregnant, she can pass the braid on to another woman who is trying to get pregnant. Another option is to do a two-part spell, creating both a braid and a talisman. The woman trying to get pregnant wears the talisman on the braided cord. Once she has a baby, she can then pass the talisman to the next woman, for whom a new braid is made. In this case, the original braid can be buried after the baby is born.

This spell sends power in waves. The female metaphor works for pregnancy, and the power is built and sent, built and sent, throughout the braiding process.

1. Begin by burning geranium-scented incense and/or having daffodils or geraniums in a vase before you. You'll need three long strands of yarn, embroidery silk, or cord: one red (for fertility), and one baby blue and the other baby pink (for babies). The ends of the cords can be knotted together and anchored to a spot—a combination of a binder clip and a heavy book can do the trick.

2. Ground and center.

3. Say, *(Name) is fertile. (Name) will have a healthy baby.*

4. This spell uses chanting and braiding to induce a trance state through repetition. Find or write a simple

song or chant that relates to fertility or birth. I used a goddess chant that called to a fertility goddess.

5. Braid and chant as long as necessary.

6. Declare success.

7. Give the braid to the person trying to get pregnant. If you used flowers, leave them on the earth as an offering.

Stuffing a Poppet

Poppets are useful for a wide variety of spells focused on people or animals. They can be used for healing, fertility, success, or—for those unconcerned about ethics—revenge. They can be used for negative magic that *is* ethical, such as containing, calming, or defusing someone who means you harm. Because making a poppet is somewhat elaborate, they are typically used for purposes that are both important and have built over time. For example, you're more likely to work on healing cancer or a chronic illness with a poppet than on healing the results of an accident. When an accident happens, you might jump into your spellwork quickly and not have time to make a poppet.

Step One: Make the Poppet

There are approximately 12,000 different ways to make a poppet. You can use the traditional technique for making a corn dolly, or you can go to a completely different tradition and make a voodoo doll. You can use commercial doll-making supplies or found materials, or buy a pre-made doll and modify it. (That's five ways. I'm guessing there are 11,995 more…)

One time, for a spell for a "crazy cat lady," we used a stuffed cat doll as the basis for a poppet, instead of one that resembled the patient. You can stitch a poppet together using photographs of the subject or the subject's actual clothing. And speaking of cat dolls, you can certainly work magic on an animal with an animal-shaped doll, if the need arises.

The only rule for making a basic magical poppet is that you must be able to open it up for stuffing. A basic cloth- or felt-based doll-making pattern will do the trick. The doll can be as simple or as elaborate as you wish. Most typically, a doll is made to resemble the subject of the spell. This can be a rough approximation: gender, skin tone, hair color and length, etc. Of course, you can get much more detailed and really make a beautiful representation.

Give special attention to the parts of the body being targeted. Suppose you're working on heart disease. You'd make sure that the heart was clearly indicated on the doll's chest.

Whichever part of the body is being worked on, leave an opening for the magical stuffing (step two). If you're working on the whole person, you can leave the entire poppet to be stuffed in ritual or choose to leave the head unstuffed (representing the mind), or the heart, or the center—however you best visualize affecting the person.

Step Two: Prepare the Stuffing

Most of the poppet can be filled with doll stuffing, cotton, rice, beans, etc., but the part you're actively working magic on should be stuffed separately.

I like to think about my ingredients list carefully. Herbs and other plant ingredients are a natural choice, but they're not the only choice. Crystals and other stones, words or phrases written on paper and folded, mementos, and other meaningful objects are all possibilities.

Let's go back to the idea of a cardiac condition. What might we stuff the chest of our poppet with?

- Healing plants, including those specific to heart disease (foxglove, sorrel, and walnut)
- Heart-shaped beads
- The Star tarot card, for health—you could use one from a tiny tarot deck or fold one up very small, or you could scan a card and shrink it digitally before printing
- Symbols of the four elements, to balance the work
- Solar symbols, for energy
- Something representing the subject—a symbol of their astrological sign, their profession, or their family, for example

Place the ingredients in a small cloth or plastic bag, and make sure the cloth or bag will fit in the space you've left in the poppet. Sewing it into the poppet will be part of the spell.

Step Three: The Spell

For the following sample spell, we'll continue with healing a heart condition. This spell, though, can be used for a variety of intentions, with appropriate changes to the wording.

This spell can be done alone or in a group. The moon phase depends on the purpose. Cardiac healing would be best done during a waxing moon, while healing cancer would be best done during a waning moon. (The goal of a healing spell in the case of cancer is most commonly to *shrink* the tumor and to *decrease* or *eliminate* metastasis; these are waning-moon functions.) Love is often the work of a full moon, and protection against evil might be best done during a dark moon.

1. Set up an altar with salt, water, incense, a censer, and your preferred magical tool (wand or athame). The altar cloth and incense should be appropriate to healing. A red altar cloth is excellent for vitality and heart health. Many incense ingredients are appropriate, including rosemary, cinnamon, cedar, hemp, sandalwood, myrrh, mint, and thyme. The poppet should be on the altar, with an opening at the heart/chest. You also need a needle and thread. The ingredient bag is also on the altar.

2. Ground and center.

3. Say, *(Name)'s open heart surgery will be successful. (Name) will recover well and be strong and healthy.*

4. Consecrate the incense: *Power of air, be here for this spell!*

5. Light the charcoal on your censer and consecrate the charcoal: *Power of fire, be here for this spell!*

6. Add incense to the censer.

7. Consecrate the salt: *Power of earth, be here for this spell!*

8. Consecrate the water: *Power of water, be here for this spell!*

9. Mix some salt into the water.

10. Say, *The powers of the elements aid me!*

11. Place your athame/wand on the poppet and say, *This poppet is (Name). (Name) is here to be healed.*

12. Pass the poppet through the smoke, saying, *(Name) is healed by fire and air.*

13. Pass the ingredient bag through the smoke, repeating, *[Name] is healed by fire and air.*

14. Wet the poppet with saltwater, saying, *(Name) is healed by water and earth.*

15. Wet the ingredient bag with saltwater, repeating, *(Name) is healed by water and earth.*

16. Place your athame/wand on the ingredient bag and say, *Healthy heart! Healthy heart! Fill (Name) with your power! Fill (Name) with your power!*

17. Place the bag in the poppet. With needle and thread, close the poppet with the healing ingredients inside. With each stitch, repeat, *Healthy heart!*

18. When the poppet is sewn up, chant, *(Name) is healed,* over and over, sending power into the poppet.

19. Say, *So mote it be. The spell is done.*

Keep the poppet on your altar. When the subject is safely home from surgery, you can give the poppet to them as a gift.

A Charm for Maintaining Your Grades

This spell helps a person maintain a specific GPA in college. This is ideal, for example, if you have scholarship money that requires a minimum GPA. This spell isn't for passing one particularly tough class or test, but to keep going at a steady pace throughout your college career.

If you got great grades in high school, then choose as your charm—as the thing you will imbue with magic—an object that represents that success, like a class ring or an honor society pin. Otherwise, a small object that represents school to you, or knowledge, or hard work, can be used. You can also choose a symbol of a god, saint, or angel. Saint Thomas Aquinas is the patron saint of students. Metatron is the archangel who is protective of students. Appropriate deities include the Hindu goddess Sarasvati and the Egyptian god Thoth. A natural stone is another option—agate, aventurine, or pumice correspond to Mercury and to successful studies.

One option with this talisman is that it could be buried. In this way, it would continue to work, protecting you from its location in the earth. However, this could be awkward for a residential college student. Most students are required to change dorms annually, so you wouldn't want to bury it in or at your dorm. I'd say a symbolic location on campus would work as a burial site for the charm, but you could also choose to wear it, which is a more traditional use of a charm. If you *do* choose to wear it, something that is an *actual* charm—something that can be worn on a chain—would be convenient. Another option would be to keep it in your desk where you study. The choice is something you can meditate on. Choose what's right for you.

The tricky thing here is not to imbue the charm with the energy of success—success is a common goal in magic, and it's not hard to figure out how to evoke it—but to give the charm the qualities of *preserving* and *maintaining steadily.*

My first thought is to use a preservative. Since salt is an ancient food preservative, it is ideal for this purpose, especially since it's a frequently used magical ingredient—one you probably already possess. Salt as a magical representative of the earth element is doubly good, because earth qualities are needed here—steadiness, stability, commitment, and longevity are all earth qualities.

We'll consecrate the charm by the four elements as usual, but we'll give the salt a dual purpose: it will work both for the preliminary elemental consecration and as a spell ingredient.

Give some thought to the incense mix as well. Success ingredients are readily available—ginger and cinnamon come to mind. What else do you need? Perseverance? Confidence? Quiet? Sobriety? Consider exactly what would help *you* maintain good grades. In addition, put yourself in the mix with something that corresponds to your astrological sign.

In both Pythagorean and Kabbalistic numerology, the numbers of importance are four and five. Four is Earth, stability, and industriousness, while five is Mercury, logic, and knowledge. Use fours and fives in the altar layout, the incense ingredients, and the words of your spoken charm. "Academic success is mine!" is a clean, clear four-word charm. You might want a different one, but this is the one we'll use here.

1. Set up an altar with your charm as well as something representative of academic success—a report card or a paper you wrote that got a great grade, a letter of recommendation, your college admission letter, etc. I'll say "paper" here. You'll need salt, water, incense, and a censer. The altar cloth should be yellow (see the list of color correspondences in appendix A).

2. Ground and center.

3. While concentrating on your goal, say, *Academic success is mine!*

4. Consecrate the incense: *Power of air, power of mind, bring thought and intelligence to my studies. Be here for this spell!*

5. Light the charcoal on your censer and consecrate the charcoal: *Power of fire, power of will, bring focus and drive to my studies. Be here for this spell!*

6. Add incense to the censer.

7. Consecrate the salt: *Power of earth, power of body, bring stability and commitment to my studies. Be here for this spell!*

8. Consecrate the water: *Power of water, power of feeling, bring intuition and insight to my studies. Be here for this spell!*

9. Mix some salt into the water.

10. Say, *Four elements, here in balance, bring power to this spell!*

11. Take the paper and wet it with the saltwater, saying four times, *By water and earth.*

12. Pass the paper through the incense smoke, saying four times, *By fire and air.*

13. Now take your charm and wet it with the saltwater, saying four times, *By water and earth.*

14. Pass the charm through the incense smoke, saying four times, *By fire and air.*

15. Lay the paper on the altar. Take five pinches of salt, placing one near each corner of the paper and one

in the center. With your hands, rub the salt into the paper, as if you were rubbing spices into a piece of meat, coating the paper with the salt, all while clearly focusing on your goal. As you do so, repeat, *Academic success is mine!*

16. Take more salt in the palm of your hand, and place the charm there. Rub your hands together, coating the charm in salt, repeating, *Academic success is mine!* over and over while you fill the charm with power.

17. Now rub the charm onto the paper, still repeating your phrase. The charm is picking up imitative power from the paper.

18. Fold the charm up into the paper. It's okay if the salt falls off the paper as this happens. The salt has done its work.

19. Say, *So mote it be.*

20. Sleep with the charm, wrapped in the paper, under your pillow. In the morning, you can put the charm on a chain and wear it continuously throughout your college career, or you can bury it or hide it as discussed previously. The paper can be kept on your desk, so it is present whenever you write or study.

Finally…

You've reached the end of this book, but since it's got "For Beginners" in the title, I hope you haven't reached the end of your studies. As you continue, I'd like you to remember a few things:

- Magic should be fun.
- Learn by doing.
- Don't be afraid to fail, and don't be afraid to try again.

There's a lifetime of learning ahead of you as a magical practitioner. In addition to practicing spellwork, you can dive more deeply into learning not just about magic but about additional occult arts that can work hand in hand with magic. This book has mentioned several, including numerology, tarot, astrology, and Kabbalah. There are also mainstream skills and knowledge that will empower you: anatomy, herbology, and mythology are just a few potential areas of study.

But most importantly, trust yourself, practice your arts, and enjoy the journey!

Tables of Correspondences

Throughout this book, I've pointed out places where knowing a correspondence (to your astrological sign, to an element, etc.) would be useful. Correspondences create a sympathetic connection. Here's a basic collection of correspondences, which your continuing studies will surely expand.

Elemental Correspondences

Air

Altar Symbols: Incense, feather, fan
Animals: Birds
Colors: White, sky blue, yellow
Magical Tools: Wand or sword/athame

Part of the Self: Mind
Part of the Body: Lungs
Elemental Beings: Sylphs
Magical Purposes: Education, communication, knowledge or wisdom, rationality, travel, legal matters, writing, new beginnings, healing the lungs or respiratory disease

Fire

Altar Symbols: Censer, candle
Animals: Lizards, snakes, big cats (lions, tigers, etc.)
Colors: Red, orange
Magical Tools: Sword/athame or wand
Part of the Self: Will
Parts of the Body: Nervous system and life force generally
Elemental Being: Salamanders
Magical Purposes: Passion, sex, strength/stamina (life force), charisma, attraction, decision-making, courage, political activism, destruction (burn out the old), exorcism, healing neurological diseases

Water

Altar Symbols: Water, seashell
Animals: Fish, crustaceans, whales, dolphins
Colors: Blue, sea green
Magical Tool: Cup
Part of the Self: Emotions
Parts of the Body: Circulatory and lymphatic systems
Elemental Beings: Undines
Magical Purposes: Dreams, love, romance, soothing, calming, psychic powers, past lives, privacy, secrecy, intuition, lactation, childbirth, healing blood or lymphatic diseases

Earth

Altar Symbols: Salt, stone, soil

Animals: Bear, pig, goat

Colors: Green, brown, black

Magical Tool: Pentacle

Part of the Self: Body

Parts of the Body: Muscle, fat, bone

Elemental Beings: Gnomes

Magical Purposes: Fertility, wealth, career, appetite, gardening, farming, marriage, home, protection, bringing things to completion/fruition, physical growth (hair growth, nail growth, healing wasting diseases or diseases related to malnourishment), healing broken bones or structural disorders

Astrological Correspondences

Aries

Dates: March 21 to April 20

Symbol: ♈

Planet: Mars

Element: Fire

Color: Red

Taurus

Dates: April 21 to May 21

Symbol: ♉

Planet: Venus

Element: Earth

Colors: Green, mauve

Gemini
Dates: May 22 to June 21
Symbol: ♊
Planet: Mercury
Element: Air
Colors: Yellow, bright colors

Cancer
Dates: June 22 to July 22
Symbol: ♋
Planet: Moon
Element: Water
Colors: Pale blue, silver

Leo
Dates: July 23 to August 22
Symbol: ♌
Planet: Sun
Element: Fire
Colors: Gold, orange, yellow

Virgo
Dates: August 23 to September 22
Symbol: ♍
Planet: Mercury
Element: Earth
Colors: Brown, navy blue, gray

Libra
Dates: September 23 to October 22
Symbol: ♎

Planet: Venus
Element: Air
Color: Pastels

Scorpio
Dates: October 23 to November 21
Symbol: ♏
Planet: Pluto
Element: Water
Colors: Burgundy, black

Sagittarius
Dates: November 22 to December 21
Symbol: ♐
Planet: Jupiter
Element: Fire
Color: Purple, royal blue

Capricorn
Dates: December 22 to January 19
Symbol: ♑
Planet: Saturn
Element: Earth
Colors: Black, brown

Aquarius
Dates: January 20 to February 19
Symbol: ♒
Planet: Uranus
Element: Air
Colors: Electric blue, rainbow

Pisces
Dates: February 20 to March 20
Symbol: ♓
Planet: Neptune
Element: Water
Colors: White, lavender, sea green

Planetary Correspondences

Sun
Symbol: ☉
Color: Yellow
Meaning: The self, vitality

Moon
Symbol: ☽
Color: Silver
Meaning: Emotions, secrets, imagination

Mercury
Symbol: ☿
Color: Orange
Meaning: Communication, rationality, learning

Venus
Symbol: ♀
Color: Green
Meaning: Romance, aesthetics, eroticism, femaleness

Mars
Symbol: ♂
Color: Red
Meaning: Aggression, courage, action, maleness

Jupiter
Symbol: ♃
Color: Blue
Meaning: Luck, optimism, expansion, justice

Saturn
Symbol: ♄
Color: Black
Meaning: Constriction, limitations, laws and rules, conscience

Uranus
Symbol: ♅
Color: Purple
Meaning: Intuition, inspiration, openness to the unusual

Neptune
Symbol: ♆
Color: Violet
Meaning: Mysticism, the unseen, illusions

Pluto
Symbol: ♇
Color: Burgundy/rust
Meaning: Power, magic, rebirth

Moon Phases

Waxing: Increase generally; anything that grows, expands, becomes
Full: Worship/theurgy, love

Waning: Decrease generally; anything that shrinks, dissipates, leaves

New: Transformation, mystery, shadow work, divination, meditation

Magical Tools

Athame

Element: Fire (sometimes air)

Meaning: The will of the practitioner, directed will, "active male"

Sword

Element: Fire (sometimes air)

Meaning: Basically the same as the athame; the sword is generally for group work, while the athame is for individual work

Wand

Element: Air (sometimes fire)

Meaning: Directed thought, power sent to the gods, "passive male"

Cup

Element: Water

Meaning: Reception, blessing, feeling, "active female"

Pentacle

Element: Earth

Meaning: Wealth, containment (as a plate), "passive female"

Color Correspondences

Red: Passion, sex, lust, life force, blood, war, aggression
Orange: Ego, materialism, pride
Yellow: Science, learning, organization
Green: Plants, agriculture, money, nature, creativity, beauty
Blue: Emotion, peace, sorrow
Indigo: Psychic arts, transcendence
Purple: Royalty, rulership, politics
Black: Death, silence, secrets
Brown: Earth, soil, animals
White: Purity, spirit
Pink: Love, friendship

Pythagorean Number Meanings

Number	Meaning
1	Initiative, leadership, courage, self, God, oneness, beginning
2	Harmony, cooperation, love, joy
3	Creativity, imagination, social connection
4	Building, practicality, industry, order
5	Freedom, sex, knowledge, games
6	Art, responsibility, family, giving
7	Occult, spirituality, research
8	Organization, authority, judgment
9	Charity, sympathy, generosity

Spell Basics

ere are the basics for you to remember—a kind of cheat
sheet to summarize what we've learned together.

Components of Magic

1. Interconnection
2. Transcending time and space
3. Intention
4. Power

Components of a Spell

1. A stated goal

2. A target

3. Intention

4. Ingredients gathered beforehand (possibly none)

5. Raising power

6. Sending power to the target

7. Finishing the spell

Sources of Power

1. Power from deity

2. Power from the self

    a. Mind: concentration, focus, meditation, trance

    b. Body: movement, dance, sex magic, pleasure, pain, aura/etheric body

    c. Mind and body jointly: rhythm, repetition, textile magic, music/sound/chants, austerities

3. Natural and supernatural sources

    a. Nature as a whole

    b. Natural things

    c. Elemental power

    d. Supernatural beings

    e. Supernatural things

4. Saved, accumulated, or stored power

    a. Magical tools

    b. History, folklore, archetypes

    c. Things used in raising power in other ways

5. Magic words: Magic words are a means of accessing power from the mind, from the body, and/or from accumulated/stored sources—depending upon the words and how they are used.

    a. Incantations, rhymes, charms, spells

    b. Calls

    c. Prayers

    d. Affirmations

    e. Barbarous words

Recommended Reading

What will further reading mean to you as a student of magic? There are so many areas to delve into!

The Beginning Magician

Let's start with more introductory books on magic. These are books that teach and explore a lot of the basics, providing core principles as well as spells to try.

Real Magic by Isaac Bonewits

This is a true classic, and indispensable. *Real Magic* is the first book to just teach *magic*—not a system of magic, not Hermetics or Golden Dawn or Hoodoo or folk tradition, but just *magic*, the underlying core that all these things have in common. Long on theory and short on spells and the like, this book is essential for expanding your mind about what you're doing and what you can do.

Spells and How They Work by Janet and Stewart Farrar
Another excellent introductory guide, this book emphasizes traditional Western magical systems, providing some introductory material on the Kabbalah, an appendix of planetary squares, and material drawn from old grimoires, while still being accessible to the beginner. There's also a chapter on sex magic.

Everyday Magic: Spells & Rituals for Modern Living by Dorothy Morrison

Earth Power: Techniques of Natural Magic by Scott Cunningham

Earth, Air, Fire & Water: More Techniques of Natural Magic by Scott Cunningham
These three books are all simple and very suited to the beginner. Scott Cunningham emphasized simplicity and naturalism in all his magic, while still being a thorough researcher. His spells are straightforward, accessible, and effective. Dorothy Morrison's book has the added advantage of providing lots of tables and resources, and she's also very modern—she doesn't leave out spells for the computer!

Encyclopedia of 5,000 Spells: The Ultimate Reference Book for the Magical Arts by Judika Illes
This is exactly what it sounds like: a big, fat volume of spells, spells, spells. There's not much in the way of instruction, but

it's a lot of fun to flip through, inspiring for your own magical work, and a trip round the world of how people do magic.

The Way of Four Spellbook: Working Magic with the Elements
by Deborah Lipp
As mentioned in the introduction, my first book on the subject of magic inspired the current volume. *The Way of Four Spellbook* digs deeply into elemental magic and presents a variety of examples, including many sample spells, using candle magic, sex magic, writing magic, dream magic, and more.

Magic and the Occult: Systems and Styles

After exploring the basics, it's time to drill down into more specific areas. Some of the following topics may become your life's study; some you may read about once and then set aside, saying, "It's not for me." Most will fall somewhere in between, but all will add to and deepen your occult knowledge and make you a better magician.

Modern Magick: Twelve Lessons in the High Magickal Arts
by Donald Michael Kraig

Modern Sex Magick: Secrets of Erotic Spirituality
by Donald Michael Kraig
Don Kraig was the first writer to make "high magic" accessible and understandable. He presented dense information in a straightforward manner that a beginner could easily grasp. By the time I read his books, I was definitely not a beginner, but I still felt that the "ceremonial" side of things was a little beyond me. Reading Don's work changed that. (By the way, I'm using quotation marks because Don didn't like to distinguish "high"

and "low" magic, and he didn't like to separate out "ceremonial" from any other kind of magic. They were all magic to him.)

Both of these books are terrific and will open the door to a lot of other magical teachers, authors, and disciplines.

Initiation into Hermetics by Franz Bardon

I'm not familiar with any "beginner" book on Hermetics. This one is a little dense, but it's indispensable. If you want to know about Hermetics, Bardon is the place to go.

Magick in Theory and Practice by Aleister Crowley

Crowley isn't easy to read, and this material is as much philosophical as practical (as the title indicates), making it even more complex. But Crowley was a true master, and eventually your magical education has to include some of his work.

How to Make and Use Talismans by Israel Regardie

Regardie was a student of Crowley's and wrote many important volumes. This is a slim little gem.

Backwoods Shamanism: An Introduction to the Old-Time American Folk Magic of Hoodoo Conjure and Rootwork by Ray "Doctor Hawk" Hess

As a contrast to the ceremonial-style books I'm offering here, this one is pure "low magic"—traditional folk magic of North America. This introduction adds a completely different set of skills to your tool chest.

The Everything Astrology Book: Discover Your True Self Among the Stars! by Trish MacGregor

Don't laugh! This is as good an introduction to astrology as you'll find anywhere, and my son and I referred back to it so often that our copy was worn almost to shreds. In fact, he took it with him when he moved out, and I *really* miss it. Given that spells throughout this book use zodiac signs and planets as sympathetic objects, this is a useful topic for you to delve into.

The Way of Four: Create Elemental Balance in Your Life
by Deborah Lipp
If you're interested in studying the four elements in depth, I happen to have written a book about that!

The Healing Craft: Healing Practices for Witches and Pagans
by Janet & Stewart Farrar and Gavin Bone
One of the things I've emphasized throughout this work is healing magic. This excellent book is the work of two long-time experts in magic and Witchcraft—the Farrars—with the input of a skilled nurse—Bone.

You Can Heal Your Life by Louise Hay
This classic of spiritual/psychic healing introduces important concepts that will be meaningful to any healer—not magic, but a way of understanding the way the psychic and the physical interact.

The Goddess and the Tree (formerly *The Witches Qabala*)
by Ellen Cannon Reed

Magic of Qabalah by Kala Trobe

Kabbalah for the Modern World
by Migene González-Wippler
These three books are smaller, introductory volumes if you're dipping your toe into Kabbalah waters. All are excellent. Ellen

Cannon Reed's book was written specifically for Wiccans who found the Kabbalah at odds with their view of Goddess religion, and were struggling to work with the two systems together.

A Garden of Pomegranates: Skrying on the Tree of Life
by Israel Regardie
For the student who has chosen to really get into the Kabbalah, this is a classic.

Reference Books

777 and Other Qabalistic Writings of Aleister Crowley
by Aleister Crowley
This is an insanely dense reference volume that corresponds everything to everything else. It can be difficult to use, but it's great to have around!

Cunningham's Encyclopedia of Magical Herbs
by Scott Cunningham

Cunningham's Encyclopedia of Crystal, Gem & Metal Magic
by Scott Cunningham

Stone Power by Dorothee L. Mella
When using herbs, gems, or minerals in a spell, I pull one or all of these three books off my shelf. Many pages are permanently bookmarked.

Wicca

Finally, here are some good books on Wicca, including my own. Although *Magical Power For Beginners* is not a Wicca book, I cannot help but reveal my bias toward it, since I've been working in a Wiccan tradition for over thirty years. If you're interested, I recommend these. Read any or all. The fun thing about these books is that the authors don't all agree about what Wicca is, so you'll be able to dig deeper, research further, and make up your own mind.

Bonewits's Essential Guide to Witchcraft and Wicca by Isaac Bonewits

The Elements of Ritual: Air, Fire, Water & Earth in the Wiccan Circle by Deborah Lipp

The Spiral Dance: A Rebirth of the Ancient Religion of the Great Goddess by Starhawk

What Witches Do: A Modern Coven Revealed by Stewart Farrar

Wicca: A Guide for the Solitary Practitioner by Scott Cunningham

Witchcraft for Tomorrow by Doreen Valiente

bibliography

Bardon, Franz. *Initiation into Hermetics*. Salt Lake City, UT: Merkur Publishing, 2001.

Bonewits, Isaac. *Bonewits's Essential Guide to Witchcraft and Wicca*. New York: Citadel Press, 2006.

———. *Neopagan Rites: A Guide to Creating Public Rituals That Work*. Woodbury, MN: Llewellyn Publications, 2007. Previously published as *Rites of Worship: A Neopagan Approach*, Earth Religions Press, 2003.

———. *Real Magic: An Introductory Treatise on the Basic Principles of Yellow Magic*. York Beach, ME: Weiser Books, 1989.

Brau, Jean-Louis, Helen Weaver, and Allan Edmands. *Larousse Encyclopedia of Astrology.* New York: New American Library, 1980.

Crowley, Aleister. *Magick in Theory and Practice.* New York: Castle Books, 1965.

———. *777 and Other Qabalistic Writings of Aleister Crowley.* San Francisco, CA: Weiser Books, 1977.

Cunningham, Scott. *Cunningham's Encyclopedia of Crystal, Gem & Metal Magic.* St. Paul, MN: Llewellyn Publications, 2001.

———. *Cunningham's Encyclopedia of Magical Herbs.* St. Paul, MN: Llewellyn Publications, 1985.

———. *Earth, Air, Fire & Water: More Techniques of Natural Magic.* St. Paul, MN: Llewellyn Publications, 2003.

———. *Earth Power: Techniques of Natural Magic.* St. Paul, MN: Llewellyn Publications, 2003.

———. *Wicca: A Guide for the Solitary Practitioner.* St. Paul, MN: Llewellyn Publications, 1988.

Dunn, Patrick. *Magic, Power, Language, Symbol: A Magician's Exploration of Linguistics.* Woodbury, MN: Llewellyn Publications, 2008.

Farrar, Janet, and Stewart Farrar. *Spells and How They Work.* Custer, WA: Phoenix Publishing, 1990.

Farrar, Janet, Stewart Farrar, and Gavin Bone. *The Healing Craft: Healing Practices for Witches and Pagans.* Blaine, WA: Phoenix Publishing, 1999.

Farrar, Stewart. *What Witches Do: The Modern Coven Revealed.* Custer, WA: Phoenix Publishing, 1989.

Filan, Kenaz, and Raven Kaldera. *Drawing Down the Spirits.* Rochester, VT: Destiny Books, 2009.

Frazer, Sir James George. *The New Golden Bough: A New Abridgment of the Classic Work.* New York: Criterion Books, 1959.

Gardner, Gerald. *Witchcraft Today.* New York: Citadel Press, 2004.

González-Wippler, Migene. *Kabbalah for the Modern World.* St. Paul, MN: Llewellyn Publications, 1987.

Hay, Louise. *You Can Heal Your Life.* London: Hay House, 1999.

Hess, Ray "Doctor Hawk." *Backwoods Shamanism: An Introduction to the Old-Time American Folk Magic of Hoodoo Conjure and Rootwork.* CreateSpace Independent Publishing, 2014.

Illes, Judika. *Encyclopedia of 5,000 Spells: The Ultimate Reference Book for the Magical Arts.* San Francisco, CA: HarperOne, 2009.

Kraig, Donald Michael. *Modern Magick: Eleven Lessons in the High Magickal Arts.* St. Paul, MN: Llewellyn Publications, 1986. Second edition, 2004.

———. *Modern Sex Magick: Secrets of Erotic Spirituality.* St. Paul, MN: Llewellyn Publications, 2003.

Lipp, Deborah. *The Elements of Ritual: Air, Fire, Water & Earth in the Wiccan Circlee.* St. Paul, MN: Llewellyn Publications, 2003.

———. *Tarot Interactions: Become More Intuitive, Psychic & Skilled at Reading Cards.* Woodbury, MN: Llewellyn Publications, 2015.

———. *The Way of Four: Create Elemental Balance in Your Life.* St. Paul, MN: Llewellyn Publications, 2004.

———. *The Way of Four Spellbook: Working Magic with the Elements.* Woodbury, MN: Llewellyn Publications, 2006.

MacGregor, Trish. *The Everything Astrology Book: Discover Your True Self Among the Stars.* Avon, MA: Adams Media Corporation, 1999.

Mella, Dorothee L. *Stone Power.* New York: Warner Books, 1986.

Morrison, Dorothy, *Everyday Magic: Spells & Rituals for Modern Living.* St. Paul, MN: Llewellyn Publications, 2001.

Reed, Ellen Cannon. *The Goddess and the Tree.* St. Paul, MN: Llewellyn Publications, 1985. Formerly *The Witches Qabala.*

Regardie, Israel. *A Garden of Pomegranates: Skrying on the Tree of Life.* St. Paul, MN: Llewellyn Publications, 1970. Third edition, 2004.

———. *How to Make and Use Talismans.* New York: Samuel Weiser, 1972.

Starhawk. *The Spiral Dance: A Rebirth of the Ancient Religion of the Great Goddess.* San Francisco, CA: Harper & Row, 1979.

Trobe, Kala. *Magic of Qabalah.* St. Paul, MN: Llewellyn Publications, 1991.

Valiente, Doreen. *An ABC of Witchcraft Past & Present,* New York: St. Martin's Press, 1973.

———. *Witchcraft for Tomorrow.* Blaine, WA: Phoenix Publications, 1988.

index

To Write to the Author

If you wish to contact the author or would like more information about this book, please write to the author in care of Llewellyn Worldwide Ltd., and we will forward your request. Both the author and the publisher appreciate hearing from you and learning of your enjoyment of this book and how it has helped you. Llewellyn Worldwide Ltd. cannot guarantee that every letter written to the author can be answered, but all will be forwarded. Please write to:

Deborah Lipp
% Llewellyn Worldwide
2143 Wooddale Drive
Woodbury, MN 55125-2989

Please enclose a self-addressed stamped envelope for reply, or $1.00 to cover costs. If outside the USA, enclose an international postal reply coupon.